Kafka's Ethics of Interpretation

Kafka's Ethics of Interpretation

Between Tyranny and Despair

✦

Jennifer L. Geddes

NORTHWESTERN UNIVERSITY PRESS
EVANSTON, ILLINOIS

Northwestern University Press
www.nupress.northwestern.edu

Printed in the United States of America

10 9 8 7 6 5 4 3 2 1

Library of Congress Cataloging-in-Publication Data

Geddes, Jennifer L., author.
Kafka's ethics of interpretation : between tyranny and despair / Jennifer L. Geddes.
pages cm
Based on the author's thesis (doctoral)—University of Virginia, 1999.
Includes bibliographical references and index.
ISBN 978-0-8101-3290-0 (cloth : alk. paper) — ISBN 978-0-8101-3289-4 (pbk. : alk. paper) — ISBN 978-0-8101-3291-7 (ebook)
1. Kafka, Franz, 1883–1924—Criticism and interpretation. I. Title.
PT2621.A26Z73297 2016
833.912—dc23

2015034917

CONTENTS

ACKNOWLEDGMENTS

It is often remarked that people tend to write about what they know or that they write out of their own neuroses, which may be two ways of saying the same thing. As one who has felt the lure of both tyranny and despair, I am grateful to the many people in this world, and to some who have departed it, who have enabled me to navigate between these two. To the many people who have contributed to the thinking and writing of this book, either directly or indirectly by their kindnesses toward me and are not named here: please forgive my failure to thank you explicitly.

It is hard to believe that this book began as my dissertation so long ago, but indeed it did, and the following people must be thanked not only for serving on my dissertation committee but also for the ongoing ways they have deepened my thinking over the years since then. Walter H. Sokel, the father of Kafka studies in the United States, guided my readings of Kafka and the writing of this work for many years. It is with deep sadness that I note that this book was submitted for publication three months after he died. I would like to think it would have given him some small measure of joy to have seen his long and generous investment of time, thought, kindness, and mentoring result in a book on Kafka so clearly indebted to his own scholarship. Larry Bouchard, once my dissertation director and now my colleague and friend, has taught me the most about interpretation and helped me to understand it as an activity of ethical and meaningful engagement with others—both textual and personal. His constant willingness to engage difficult questions and others' confusions with generosity and kindness is a model I hope always to strive to follow. James Davison Hunter introduced me to Pierre Bourdieu's work and to theories of power, but more important he believed in my worth as a scholar and colleague, long before I imagined myself to be either, and I am grateful for the many ways he has supported my education and my career. Peter Ochs deepened my knowledge of Jewish thought, particularly Levinas's work, and drew me into the world of Jewish studies with his welcome and encouragement.

In addition to these excellent readers, among others, the book benefited from the editing skills of Emily Gravett and Kristine Harmon and the attentive reading and thoughtful responses of Slavica Jakelić, Charles Mathewes, Maruta Ray, and Joshua Yates, who read all or portions of the book. The book also benefited from the patience with which Henry L. Carrigan, my editor at Northwestern University Press, awaited the manuscript and the kind encouragement with which he responded to my emails.

Many friends have traveled with me through the many years this book was in the making—a book that is implicitly about ways to navigate the loneliness of life by engaging with others. I will name just a few of the many who should be thanked: Lisa Landes, my oldest friend; Connally Gilliam and Karin Voth Harmon, friends through spiritual and intellectual journeys that continue to this day; Anne McIlhaney, my fellow traveler through graduate school and motherhood and all the stages in between; and Saphira Baker, Slava Jakelić, Jason Varsoke, Josh Yates, and Molly Yates, without whom the last decade would have been much lonelier and much less fun.

Although Kafka's works do not readily suggest reasons to feel deep gratitude toward family members, my own life certainly does, and I cannot imagine having made it through to the end of this book, much less this far in life, without the gifts they have given and continue to give to me. Ted and Ethel Fugler, my grandparents now departed, were anchors of love in my life before and during the writing of this book. My aunt and uncle, Dorothy and Keith Johnson; my father, Gary Geddes, and his wife, Ann Eriksson; my stepmother Jan Jeffers and her husband, Mal Jeffers; my sisters Bronwen and Sarcy Geddes—all have encouraged me along the path with good humor and love. My daughter, Isabelle Mathewes, with her thoughtful reflection, and my son, Henry Mathewes, with his exuberance, have brought joy I did not imagine possible. Chuck Mathewes, whose love of life and laughing and learning often moves me beyond my tendency toward microscopic myopia, is both the paradigm of a generous colleague and a wonderful husband—I still cannot believe my luck in marrying him.

There is one more person to thank: my mother, to whom this book is dedicated. Nowhere is the inadequacy of language, the incompleteness of my words, more obvious to me than in my efforts to thank her . . . for everything. I dedicate this book to Norma Geddes, who is the most generous and kind person I know and at the same time a model for how to live life with passion and an appetite for all the joys and pleasures life has to offer, and without whom the world would seem dull and gray.

Kafka's Ethics of Interpretation

INTRODUCTION

In his essay "Franz Kafka: Notes on the Tenth Anniversary of His Death," Walter Benjamin tells us that Kafka "took all conceivable precautions against the interpretation of his writings."[1] Theodor Adorno declares "each sentence says 'interpret me,' and none will permit it."[2] Harold Bloom argues that Kafka "did everything possible to evade interpretation."[3] More recently Clayton Koelb has described Kafka as "a writer who made a career out of resisting interpretation."[4] These are just a few of the most recognizable names among a whole chorus of critics who declare that Kafka resisted or purposely evaded interpretation. This book argues that they are all wrong and not only that they are wrong but also that their claims about Kafka's deliberate uninterpretability misconstrue a central concern of his work. Kafka was not trying to avoid, evade, or prevent interpretation; rather, his works are centrally concerned with it. They depict, articulate, and elicit interpretation. It is the activity his characters undertake more than any other, and their success or failure at it carries life-or-death consequences. Kafka's depictions of interpretation in his stories suggest a range of ways we might interpret his works—some he might well resist but others that he, in fact, engages in himself and elicits from his readers. To claim that he wrote in such a way as to evade interpretation reveals both a reductive view of interpretation and a failure to pay attention to what his works tell us about it.

In this book, I aim to show that attention to the interpretive activity that takes place in and in response to Kafka's works both enriches and deepens our engagement and understanding of his works, on the one hand, and, on the other, tells us something about ourselves and how we might live more fully in this world. Naomi Schor suggests a similar approach when she writes, "Via the interpretant [the interpreting character] the author is trying to tell the interpreter something *about* interpretation and the interpreter would do well to listen and take note."[5] By reading Kafka in this way, we see more in his works than we would otherwise and are challenged to think about the ways we read texts, engage others, and navigate the world through our interpretations of them. Kafka's ethics of interpretation has something to say about his engagement with the cultural and historical contexts in which he found himself, the very movements of characters in his texts, and the relation of his readers to the world in which they find themselves. I am not proposing that this is the only, or even the best, way to read Kafka's works; rather, attention to the interpretation that takes place within and in response to his works suggests a way of reading that allows room for multiple interpretations, new discoveries with each rereading, deepening understanding over time, and an affirmation of the rich possibilities for new interpretations of Kafka's works with each new generation of readers and in new cultural and historical contexts.

In addition to arguing that Kafka's works do not resist interpretation, but rather invite it, I also want to suggest that in doing so they call us to reconsider what we mean by interpretation. Kafka's texts invite a reinterpretation of interpretation. They depict the dangers and violence of engaging in interpretation as an activity of decipherment by which we aim to grasp the "one true meaning" of a text. I argue that in reading the battles of interpretation that take place in Kafka's texts, we are led to the possibility of reenvisioning interpretation as a way in which to engage a text in all its complexity, ambiguity, and plurality.

The preponderance of statements about the impossibility of interpreting Kafka, and the claims that Kafka resists interpretation, are important to note because they themselves are part of the story of Kafka's ethics of interpretation. Kafka's works reveal a hermeneutical drive in their readers, a strong desire for singular, complete, and definitive interpretations—a desire that often grows stronger the more it finds itself unable to achieve its ends. Sometimes this desire can be fulfilled, particularly when what is confronted takes the form of a problem to be solved. But as Kafka himself notes, "life is more than a . . . puzzle,"[6] and often the very things that most arouse our desire for a complete interpretation are those things least amenable to it, such as literary texts, other people, the world, ourselves. Confronted with a complex text, such as Kafka's literary works, that we cannot interpret definitively, for which we cannot claim to have completed interpretation, we sometimes depict that complexity, multivocality, or plurality as resistance or evasion. But this depiction says more about the nature of our own efforts at understanding than about the text itself. It functions as a way to avoid facing the limits of our interpretive capacities.

The suggestion of resistance or evasion on the part of Kafka himself or his text characterizes the relationship between Kafka or his text and the reader as a battle for power, as the interpreter seeking to interpret the text and either the text or Kafka resisting or evading that effort. This depiction has inspired other scholars to defend Kafka's works against the violent impositions of interpreters.[7] But in both versions of "the battle for power"—whether the Kafkan text is resisting interpretation or the critic is defending the Kafkan text against the gangs of interpreters—the activity of interpretation seems to remain the same. It is the means by which the reader captures the meaning, unlocks the gate, solves the puzzle. Either the text resists this effort of the critic, or the critic must defend the text (or Kafka) against these efforts.

Susan Sontag offers such a view of interpretation when she declares that "to interpret is to impoverish, to deplete the world."[8] She points to Kafka criticism as exemplary in its violence against the text:

> The work of Kafka, for example, has been subjected to a mass ravishment by no less than three armies of interpreters. Those who read Kafka as a social allegory see case studies of the frustrations and insanity of modern bureaucracy and its ultimate issuance in the totalitarian state. Those who read Kafka as a psychoanalytic allegory see desperate revelations of Kafka's fear of his father. . . . Those who read Kafka as a religious allegory explain that K. in *The Castle* is trying to gain access to heaven, that Josef K in *The Trial* is being judged by the inexorable and mysterious justice of God.[9]

The interpretations she enumerates might be reductive if they claimed to be complete interpretations of his work, but might it not be reductive to say that these interpretations constitute ravishments of the text?[10]

Much hinges on the claims one makes for one's interpretation. J. Hillis Miller suggests that it is the claim to "have Kafka right" rather than the plurality of interpretations that is problematic when he refers to the "distressingly contradictory ways of reading Kafka that have developed over the years. Readings of many different kinds—religious readings, autobiographical readings, psychoanalytical readings, political readings, sociological readings, intrinsic readings and allegorical readings—have proliferated, each claiming to 'have Kafka right.' "[11] Implicit in Sontag's assertions is the idea that to interpret Kafka's work is not only potentially an exhausted task but also a morally questionable one, a kind of ravishment. But why is a Kafkan text considered "ravished" by these interpretations of it? And why are interpreters considered to be "armies"? The presentation of Kafka's works as victims of their interpreters suggests they are vulnerable to, and endangered by, interpretation. Are they really so frail? Might they not be eliciting these interpretations, rather than suffering because of them?

Interpretation need not be the violating activity Sontag describes it to be. Sontag is right in pointing out the dangers of interpretation, but she mistakes these dangers for interpretation's very essence. There are interpretations that claim to define their objects, to have grasped them, to have definitively interpreted them, but might we not see these as revealing the temptations of interpreters rather than the nature of interpretation? So this book argues through an exploration of Kafka's works, which are themselves explorations of interpretive activities. For not only are they fertile ground for the occasion of interpretation on the part of the thousands of critics who have written about Kafka, they also provide fertile content for thinking about interpretation and examining our own interpretive efforts in response to his works.

I am suggesting that Kafka's texts call us to rethink the activity of interpretation itself: to see it not as decipherment but as engagement, not as solving a puzzle but as seeking to understand better, not as a violence against the text but as a response to its invitation to interpret in a different way. Interpretation can be seen as the effort to glimpse the "lively, changing face of truth," to use an image Kafka presented in a letter to his translator and lover, Milena Jesenská. This way of interpreting requires that the interpreter relinquish the goal of complete interpretation and acknowledge that there is always more than what one can decipher. This is not to deny that interpretation can be reductive or violent, but interpretation of that sort is itself reductive of what interpretive activity can be and, it is crucial to note, brings an end to the process of interpretation by claiming to have completed it.

In other words, I am arguing that Kafka's texts do not avoid or resist interpretation; they invite it, but they do so in a way that reveals the fantasies of definitive interpretation and desires for completion with which we often approach texts. We redescribe the richness, plurality, complexity, and changing nature of his texts as resistance or evasion of interpretation rather than explore the reductive modes by which we approach them. Why do we expect his works to have the same kind of ontology as puzzles that can be solved? Why are they seen as resisting interpretation when we are not able to make simple sense of them? We would not think to say that the number pi resists interpretation because we cannot complete the sequence of numbers to which it refers. Rather, we understand that this infinite sequence of digits revises an understanding of numbers as a discrete and closed set of numerical items, as we may have conceived of them when we were first learning about numbers. The number pi brings into sharp focus an infinity that always exceeds our efforts to grasp it, that brings into view the horizon of our numerical view. We know there are always more digits. The further we go in identifying the digits, the further the horizon moves. In learning about numbers, the child's proud declarations to be able to count to ten, then twenty, then one hundred turn to questions like, "What comes after a million . . . a billion . . . a trillion?" until she understands that numbers exceed our capacity to name or count them.

My argument is that Kafka's works suggest a similar movement for our understanding of interpretation: from seeing it as the pursuit of the one, true meaning or a finite set of meanings to a way of engaging and navigating the texts, people, and world we encounter; from something through which we seek to achieve completion and mastery to an activity in which we acknowledge our own limits and incapacities, as well as temptations. In reading Kafka's texts, we move from decipherment to dialogue, understood in the rich sense of an interaction that is vigorous and challenging; from finding the key or capturing *the* meaning to something more akin to reaching approximations, deepening understandings, and catching glimpses. But his works also enable us to recognize the temptations to violence, on the one hand, and despair, on the other, with which our efforts to interpret must always contend.

This sense of interpretation finds parallels in numerous places, from the early traditions of rabbinic interpretation in Judaism to contemporary theory. Interpretive activity is central to all we do as scholars, no matter what our discipline. It is also central to much of what we do as humans in the world, societies, communities, relationships with others, and even in relation to ourselves. In order to situate this work in relation to other efforts to understand interpretation both in its temptations and possibilities, I want to highlight recent trends in Kafka scholarship and how this book differs from them in what I hope are fruitful ways. I then identify two conversations, broadly conceived, outside Kafka scholarship with parallels to the present study: rabbinic interpretation and Jewish hermeneutics, on the one hand, and, on the other, contemporary theory that attends to the ways in which interpretive practices are inextricably linked to forms of power, violence, and suffering.

Recent Trends in Kafka Criticism

Recent trends in literary studies have drawn our attention to the ways in which particular cultural streams have influenced literary works, whether they be related to gender, ethnicity, cultural productions, and the like. Recent Kafka scholarship has focused on Kafka's life, with several biographies and studies drawing out unexamined aspects of his historical and cultural contexts. This is not a new focus. For example, Evelyn Torton

Beck argued over forty years ago for the important influence of Yiddish theater on Kafka and his writing, and biographies of Kafka have appeared with some regularity over a long period. But recent work has intensified this focus on the biographical and cultural contexts of Kafka's works and brought important aspects of his life and world to light. For example, Stanley Corngold, Jack Greenberg, and Benno Wagner's *Franz Kafka: The Office Writings* dispels the picture of Kafka as a low-level bureaucrat and reveals that far from being a reclusive failure, Kafka was both an important official in the Workmen's Accident Insurance Institute and engaged in significant legal cases concerning workers' rights. John Zilcosky has examined Kafka's interest in travel writing and explored the themes of travel, colonies, the exotic, as well as metaphorical journeys in Kafka's work in *Kafka's Travels: Exoticism, Colonialism, and the Traffic of Writing*, and Hanns Zischler's *Kafka Goes to the Movies* searches out the movies Kafka attended and unpacks their influence on his work.[12]

Other recent books have focused specifically on Kafka's relation to Jewish culture, building on Ritchie Robertson's earlier *Kafka: Judaism, Politics, and Literature*. For example, Iris Bruce's *Kafka and Cultural Zionism: Dates in Palestine* gives a detailed account of the influence on Kafka of Jewish texts, cultural performances, and individuals with whom he came in contact. June O. Leavitt's *The Mystical Life of Kafka* extends beyond Jewish mysticism and Kafka's interest in Kabbalah to include other spiritual, mystical, and occult movements of the time.[13] Vivian Liska's *When Kafka Says We: Uncommon Communities in German-Jewish Literature* explores the notions of community in Kafka's work, and the work of other German-Jewish authors of the time, and argues that their "marginal position generates unconventional literary approaches toward communities and selves and the relationship between them . . . and from a variety of standpoints they formulate a critique of closed communal entities as well as the myths, traditions, and beliefs by which such communities legitimize themselves."[14] Most recently Manfred Engel and Ritchie Robertson's edited volume *Kafka und die Religion in der Moderne: Kafka, Religion, and Modernity* marks the deepening turn to religion in Kafka studies and helps to situate the study of Kafka and religion in richer understandings of the broader contexts of religious life and belief in early twentieth-century Europe.[15]

Critics have long shown an interest in the details of Kafka's life, but a slew of new Kafka biographies in the past decade suggests an intensification of focus on Kafka himself. Some biographies have appeared in introductory series, such as Ritchie Robertson's *Kafka* and his *Kafka: A Very Short Introduction*, Sander L. Gilman's *Franz Kafka*, and Saul

Friedländer's *Franz Kafka: The Poet of Shame and Guilt.*[16] Other recent, and more substantial, biographies include Reiner Stach's two volumes, *Kafka: The Decisive Years* and *Kafka: The Years of Insight*, and Nicholas Murray's *Kafka: A Biography.*[17] Both Stach's and Murray's biographies offer a wealth of information, dispel Kafka stereotypes, and paint a rich picture, with finely drawn strokes, of Kafka and his works.

The focus on the particularity of Kafka's cultural, historical, and religious contexts has deepened our understanding of the world in which Kafka lived, and the numerous biographies of the past decade have vastly increased our understanding of Kafka himself, but they have also drawn our attention away from the works themselves.[18] Not completely away, of course: several of the mentioned studies offer readings of Kafka's works enlightened by the cultural context or biographical portrait they paint; many provide insight into Kafka's works by drawing out their cultural references and literary precursors or models. But I would like to suggest that Kafka's own central concern with interpretive activity and his sense of it as having life-or-death consequences have been neglected in recent trends of Kafka scholarship.[19] This book attempts not to "fill the gap," a move that would be antithetical to the tenor of this work, but rather to suggest that attention to the interpretive activity in Kafka's works has much to teach us about those works, as well as ourselves and the world in which we live.

As will become apparent in the course of the book, I am not claiming that attention to interpretation is *the key* to Kafka's works. The long quest for *the key* has led to a rich cornucopia of interpretations of Kafka's works, but it has also suggested that the space of Kafka interpretations is a zero-sum kind of game in which someone, eventually, will find *the key* that will unlock the gate and bring the whole game to completion. Even as perceptive a reader as Benjamin searches for such a key (though he recognizes that such a key is beyond his grasp); he writes to Gershom Scholem, "I think the key to Kafka's work is likely to fall into the hands of the person who *is able to extract the comic aspects from Jewish theology.*"[20] Instead of seeing interpretation as the process by which one finds the key that will unlock the whole mystery, I am arguing, with the help of Kafka himself, for a reconsideration of interpretation as an activity that can take many forms—some that lead to violence and suffering and others that offer the possibility of living in the world in resistance to such violence. Interpretation can take the form of the effort to find the one, true meaning of a text, which often becomes the imposition of a meaning onto the text, and it can take the form of a deeply attentive engagement with the text that at the same time acknowledges the limits of its capacity to fathom the text and allows for multiple possible interpretations—the intimacy and intensity of the engagement does not take the form of exclusivity. I hope my study of Kafka's works will be interpreted in such a manner and as itself interpreting in such a manner. The picture of interpretation I am drawing here, both in the critique of its violent possibilities and in the proposal of it as a form of ethical engagement in the world, finds parallels in both rabbinic interpretive practices and contemporary theory.

Rabbinic Interpretation and Jewish Hermeneutics

As noted, Kafka's Judaism has been the subject of many critical works, whether focusing on his cultural contexts, his religious heritage, or his Jewish identity.[21] Kafka's identity as a Jew, his engagement with Jewish culture and texts, his interest in Yiddish theater and interactions with the actors, and his long-standing conversations with his Zionist friends all meant that he was swimming in the intellectual, cultural, and historical waters of Judaism. However, I want to draw on the connection between Kafka's writings and Jewish textual and interpretive traditions rather than tracing the influence of Judaism or Jewish cultural productions on Kafka.[22] Kafka's works have been connected with both Kabbalah, esoteric Jewish mysticism, on the one hand, and, on the other, midrash, rabbinic interpretive practices used to elucidate Hebrew scripture.

Gershom Scholem, the most important twentieth-century scholar of Kabbalah, saw Kafka's work as a form of secularized Kabbalah, and Karl Grözinger has written a whole book on the connections between Kafka and Kabbalah, describing Scholem's characterization of Kafka's works as "a secularized representation of the kabbalistic conception of the world."[23] Harold Bloom draws contemporary readers into that web of influence by declaring that "our understanding of Kabbalah is Kafkan anyway, since Kafka profoundly influenced Gershom Scholem, and no one will be able to get beyond Scholem's creative or strong misreading of Kabbalah for decades to come. I repeat this point to emphasize its shock value: we read Kabbalah, via Scholem, from a Kafkan perspective."[24] But it is not the mysticism of Kabbalah but rather the hermeneutic practices of midrash, the rabbinic form of interpretation that seeks out the gaps and spaces in the Hebrew bible, that is most illuminating in thinking about Kafka's ethics of interpretation.

Kafka's focus on interpretation as an ongoing mode of engagement that resists hermeneutical tyranny mirrors rabbinic interpretive practices. Iris

Bruce claims that "Kafka found Talmudic discourse fascinating" and cites Kafka's own recognition of his capacities for Talmudic discourse when he describes himself, in a diary entry, as having argued in a "Talmudic style" with his friend Hugo Bergmann.[25] Rabbinic interpretation is characterized by multiple interpretations existing side by side in conversation and argumentation: one rabbi commenting on a previous rabbi's exegesis and awaiting commentary by subsequent rabbinic commentaries. James Kugel argues that midrash is "not just dry biblical commentary: it is clever, inventive, quite down-to-earth, sometimes humorous, often moving, and always full of fresh insights with regard to the biblical text."[26] Daniel Boyarin points to the distinctive nature of midrashic interpretation, or, rather, the several kinds of interpretation that can be found in midrash: "The interpretations found in these several works [midrash] are manifold in nature, but all of them are more or less different from the commentary of the European traditions in that they do not seem to involve the privileged pairing of a signifier with a specific set of signifieds. It is perhaps this characteristic that has rendered midrash so fascinating to some recent literary critics."[27] In contrast to forms of thought that seek a singular, unitary, and knowable truth, in Talmudic discourse "consensus and dissent coexist, the laws of reason are sufficiently flexible to accommodate both constancy and change, and unending argument results."[28]

Kafka's works perform this argumentative openness. By depicting battles between different modes of interpretation—hermeneutical tyranny and hermeneutical impotence or despair—Kafka reveals their inherent violence, but in that revelation he enacts or performs a different kind of interpretive activity, one that keeps open the space of interpretation, rejects closure and completion as violent, but also rejects the escape of despair. Like midrash, Kafka's work is necessarily multivocal and dialogical, argumentative, seeking the truth but recognizing that task as an ongoing one that can never be completed. The temptations to tyranny and to despair are always proximate in midrash and in Kafka's works, but persistence in the activity of interpretation is itself a means by which to resist those temptations. Interpretation as an ongoing, never-finished activity breaks open the frozen ground of "complete interpretation," providing a way out of its solid tyranny. When Kafka proposes that books should be like axes for the frozen sea within us, he suggests a vivid image of this breaking open of the space that hermeneutical tyranny encloses. But interpretive activity is both critique and ethical engagement; interpretation also tethers one to the text, the world, others, oneself in such a way as to resist the despair that can ensue in the face of hegemonic interpretive power.[29]

Connections with Contemporary Theory

This double character of critique and ethical engagement, of resistance and close attention, has parallels in recent theoretical approaches to literature and culture, from the later deconstructive readings of Jacques Derrida, in which we see a more explicit turn to ethical concerns, to the philosophical studies of power and identity in Judith Butler and to the political meditations of Giorgio Agamben. The charges of ethical irresponsibility and elitist abstraction leveled at late twentieth-century theory have grown quieter (at least in some places) as leading figures have begun to attend to the ethical implications of their work.[30] For example, Judith Butler's *Giving an Account of Oneself*, which features Kafka's drawings on the cover, offers an ethical meditation on agency, identity, and responsibility.[31] By exposing the cracks in seemingly comprehensive totalities and reading authoritative texts against themselves, critical theory creates space in which previously marginalized and silenced voices are able to speak—a movement particularly important in postcolonial and gender theory. These voices have brought to attention a whole range of ethical issues, experiences of suffering, and aspects of human experience that have previously garnered inadequate attention, and they have also suggested the importance of thinking about new ways of interpreting, ways that allow for multiple voices and different views, are self-critical and modest in their claims to truth, are open to the possibilities of critique and revision, and yet do not devolve into a relativistic nihilism or despair—ways of interpreting that echo Kafka's ethics of interpretation.

Quoting Kafka's character Red Peter in "A Report to the Academy," Anke Snoek, in *Agamben's Joyful Kafka*, sees in the idea of a "way out" the basis for picturing a different Kafka than the despairing loner he is sometimes depicted as being, a Kafka who moves in the space created by a critique of tyranny and a resistance to despair: "Although at first glance, Agamben and Kafka appear to be groping blindly in their lack of consolation, it appears to be precisely the notion of a way out that connects them and that is so difficult at times to square with the darkness of their work."[32] This way out offers, according to Snoek, "freedom, potentiality and possibilities to withdraw from power."[33] In fact, Agamben suggests that Kafka is "the author not only of hopelessness, but also of hope; he does not only describes [*sic*] how we are subordinated by law, but also strategies to find freedom beyond this subordination."[34] Beth Hawkins also sees this possibility for affirmation in Kafka, whom she describes as a "reluctant theologian" and his writings as a "covenantal midrash"; his exegetical method, she argues, "*both* strives to unmask and expose the raw tendencies that are responsible for illusion-construction *and* looks to give voice to the plenitude of meaning in a text . . . a restorative hermeneutics."[35]

Kafka, she argues, "reject[s] the totalizing impulse, and instead choose[s] literary forms that reflect a pervasive anti-systematicity, a vehement refusal of closure or finality."[36] What I am suggesting here is that Kafka's ethics of interpretation is a "way out" of the grip of hermeneutical tyranny, but one that does not give in to the temptation of the "way out" offered by despair—it navigates the space between them.

Thus, the very facets of Kafka's work with parallels in midrash also suggest parallels in work in critical theory, poststructuralism, psychoanalytic and feminist theory, and cultural studies. Critiques of hegemonic power and interpretive violence, proposals of destabilized meaning and the impossibility of closure, recognition of plurivocality and the contingency of our readings—all have characterized the efforts of thinkers like Theodor Adorno, Michel Foucault, Gilles Deleuze, Jacques Derrida, Giorgio Agamben, Judith Butler, Julia Kristeva, and others. These critiques and proposals are also crucial to Kafka's works. But rather than seeing interpretation itself as a mechanism of hegemonic power, as Deleuze and Félix Guattari proclaim—"We believe only in a Kafka *politics* that is neither imaginary nor symbolic. We believe only in one or more Kafka *machines* that are neither structure nor phantasm. We believe only in a Kafka *experimentation* that is without interpretation or significance and rests only on the tests of experience."[37]—I argue that interpretive activity is itself the very means for breaking open and resisting that power. Interpretive activity is not the problem. In fact, it is when interpretation *stops*, by the claim to have completed interpretation or to be in possession of *the truth*, that tyranny begins, rather than the other way around.

The Structure of the Book

In the chapters that follow I offer close readings of four key Kafka texts in which Kafka himself focuses intently on interpretation, in order to draw out what I call his ethics of interpretation. The works discussed here—Kafka's "Letter to His Father," "The Judgment," "The Metamorphosis," and "In the Penal Colony"—depict battles of interpretation between a hermeneutical tyrant and his impotent subject, battles that result in the death of the protagonist but also suggest ways out of that battle and alternatives to both tyranny and despair. These stories depict the violent potential of interpretation at the same time that they show the destructive consequences of failing to engage in it. Somewhere between tyranny and despair, we must find a way to read and interpret Kafka's works. Somewhere between tyranny and despair, we might find a way to live.

Each of the four chapters of the book proceeds by way of a close reading of one of Kafka's works, which is then put in conversation with a theorist who pursues similar concerns. Kafka's works shed light on Sigmund Freud's *Interpretation of Dreams*, Pierre Bourdieu's theories of power, Tzvetan Todorov's presentation of the genre of the fantastic, and Emmanuel Levinas's essay "Useless Suffering," while their theories help to illuminate aspects of Kafka's fiction. What is avoided is yet another application to Kafka's works of some theory that then claims to have unlocked their secret. By seeking to move dialogically between a textually grounded exploration of the connections between interpretation, power, violence, and suffering in Kafka's works, on the one hand, and theoretical explorations of these themes, on the other, I hope to show that it is possible to bring ethics, fiction, and theory into conversation in a way that does not privilege theory or apply it like a deciphering device for literature but rather enhances our reading and interpretive activity. For Kafka's fictions are themselves explorations of the ethics of interpretation and theories of power; they question hermeneutic strategies of violence and justifications of suffering. Reading Kafka, Freud, Bourdieu, Todorov, and Levinas together makes aspects of their works visible and more proximate than they otherwise would be without this effort at dialogic reading—or at least this is what I hope to show.

Two questions might arise from this initial description of the structure of the book: Why these four short works of Kafka's and not, for example, his more well-known, unfinished novels? Why these four theorists, who certainly make a somewhat eclectic group, at least in terms of their disciplinary homes if not their geographical or temporal locations? The four works of Kafka's read here include a highly stylized letter—as much a work of literary composition as any in his oeuvre: in fact, Reiner Stach describes it as a "core text of literary modernity"[38]—and three short stories that were published in Kafka's lifetime and that are among, if not the, most important stories Kafka wrote. Kafka saw a deep connection between "The Judgment" and "The Metamorphosis," which is evidenced by the fact that he suggested to his publisher that the two be published together with "The Stoker" under the title *Die Söhne* (*The Sons*).[39] Even more important for arguing a connection between the three stories under consideration here is Kafka's later comment, in October of 1915, that he had wanted the three to be published together under the title *Strafen* (*Punishments*).[40] Kafka's "Letter to His Father" fits naturally with the connections between the stories concerning punishments, patriarchal power, and sons. Though it was written after the stories, it lays out and performs the interpretive modes that Kafka represents in his stories.

In response to the question about why these four theorists, there is nothing that obviously links them together, and in two cases—Bourdieu and Levinas—even the link with Kafka is not immediately clear. Indeed, four other theorists could have been chosen—there is no suggestion of necessity here. Instead, these four are the theorists who, when I read them, made me think more deeply about Kafka's stories, and thinking about those stories helped me to understand their theoretical works better—helped me to understand better, specifically, Freud's oscillation between his claims to have completed interpretation and his acknowledgment that there is always something unfathomable in dreams; Bourdieu's identification of different kinds of capital and their role in the struggle for power; Todorov's identification of hesitation as the defining feature of the fantastic, but then his falling prey to the temptation to resolve that hesitation, even in his very discussion of it in relation to Kafka's "The Metamorphosis"; and the gap between Levinas's dense phenomenology of suffering and his discussion of the end of theodicy. Kafka's stories helped me articulate an unease I felt in reading their works, an unease that related to a tension, contradiction, or gap in these theorists' works. And I hope to show that the theories, in turn, help us to read Kafka's stories more attentively.

In the first chapter, through a close reading of his "Letter to His Father," I unpack Kafka's presentation of the different modes of interpretation he and his father use, specifically the hermeneutical tyranny of his father, the hermeneutical impotence of Kafka as his son, and the mode of interpretation that he himself performs as the writer of the letter. While his father sees things as simple, accepts no other views but his own, and interprets like a tyrant whose authority rests on his person rather than the validity or accuracy of his interpretations, Kafka presents himself as the impotent subject, the voiceless and cowering son. And yet Kafka as the writer of the letter performs and thereby offers a different hermeneutical mode from either the hermeneutical tyrant or his impotent subject—one that recognizes complexity without trying to simplify it, allows for plurality instead of reducing everything to a single view, and accepts contingency and the possibility of change over time. This articulation of different modes of interpretation—and the different views of the world and the things in it that these modes of interpretation represent—is then used to read a moment in Sigmund Freud's *Interpretation of Dreams*, where he vacillates between the claim to have completed an interpretation of a dream and the suggestion that all dreams have some central point, or "navel," that is uninterpretable. Both Freud and Kafka point to a mode of interpretation that moves within the space between the tyranny of claiming to have completed interpretation of what cannot be completely interpreted and the despair of being unable to interpret anything at all, and point to the possibility of an ethics of interpretation as a mode of engaging in the world.

The biographical battle between father and son, depicted in the "Letter to His Father," is condensed in fictional form in "The Judgment." Kafka's own favorite work, "The Judgment" offers a powerful illustration of the connections between interpretation and power. The story with its locomotive pace has bewildered many, including Kafka himself, but in chapter 2, I show how Bourdieu's disaggregation of forms of capital illuminates why Kafka's protagonist Georg Bendemann, who begins the morning on the brink of yet more success, ends up dead in a river. In his confrontation with his father, Georg finds that each form of capital he has gained is reinterpreted as his father's success and source of power, until finally Georg, bereft, is sentenced to death by drowning by his father. Interpretations serve as both the weapons of the battle and that over which the battle is taking place. As with Kafka's own father, the hermeneutical tyranny of Georg's father is not complete, despite his declarations of power and claims to have both Georg's friend and mother on his side: in his death, Georg asserts an identity that refutes his father's declaration that he is a devilish human being. Though he pays with his life, Georg regains a measure of agency by which he resists his father's hermeneutical tyranny.

The instability of identity that is so evident by the end of "The Judgment" is apparent at the very beginning of "The Metamorphosis." Chapter 3 moves from the discussion of power and interpretation of chapter 2 to a closer look at the processes of definition and categorization involved in interpretation. The status we give to the definitions and categories we use have radical consequences, as the declaration that Gregor is "not Gregor" by his sister reveals. A seemingly impossible task is required to avoid doing violence to Gregor's identity: he must be seen as both human and bug while resisting the temptation to simplify these two identities into one. Tzvetan Todorov's discussion of the genre of the fantastic proves illuminating not only for his discussion of "The Metamorphosis" as an example of the fantastic but also for how his own reading of the story fails to resist the very temptation that needs to be resisted for the fantastic to be maintained. Parallels between the critic and the characters in the story suggest a broader relevance for how we think about the whole activity of interpretation in the face of those things that resist the categories by which we make sense of them, that require either new categories or the juxtapositional maintenance of two categories that usually oppose each other.

The fourth chapter explores one of Kafka's most difficult stories, "In the Penal Colony." By reading the story in tandem with Levinas's equally difficult (though in different ways) essay "Useless Suffering," aspects of each text are illuminated. Central to each is the question of how we interpret the suffering of others, whether they be the radically other of the criminal or the uncomfortably close other of the neighbor. The officer of the penal colony presents a narrative of meaningful torture that includes descriptions of pain, but he fails to respond to that pain in any way that might suggest he understands it as suffering. Levinas begins his essay with a phenomenology of suffering that serves as a stark contrast to the officer's depiction of pain. The two can be read as counterphenomenologies, striking in the ways that they each describe processes of inscription and the relationship of bodily pain and meaning but do so in diametrically opposed ways. Levinas presents suffering as the experience of the refusal of meaning; Kafka's officer, in contrast, waxes eloquent about the prisoner's ability to decipher the law through his wounds and the community's sense that justice is being done. The explorer listening to the officer's account serves as a model for the reader, revealing one way in which we might read the officer's narrative. But both Kafka and Levinas point to other ways of reading and responding to such narratives and to the suffering they justify, ways that recognize the infliction of suffering as something to be prevented or halted rather than justified and interpreted as meaningful.

Through these close readings of Kafka's works, in which a battle between the hermeneutical tyrant and his impotent subject ends in destruction, a different mode of interpretation emerges, one that we might understand as Kafka's reinterpretation of interpretation. Rather than an activity of mastery like solving a puzzle, interpretation becomes, for Kafka, a means of navigating and engaging the complexity of others and the world. Rather than something that finds its endpoint in a solution, interpretation becomes an ongoing activity, one that never ends, and its "arrivals" at meaning and understanding are always open to revision and aware of their provisionality.

Kafka's ethics of interpretation entails a certain vision of the world. "Life," he writes to his father, "is more than a puzzle"; that is, it is more complex than the kind of thing one can figure out and solve like a jigsaw puzzle. There are multiple views of the world; one view cannot capture it. People are not amenable to complete interpretations: they are more complicated; they change over time. To try to contain the complexity, changes, and multiplicity of something in what one presumes to be a complete interpretation is to misread it and possibly to do violence to it.

In short, Kafka's ethics of interpretation emerges from his understanding of the nature of things; hermeneutics follows from ontology.

Benjamin offers a vivid illustration of the way in which Kafka's works call for a different kind of reading than one that would decipher a clear and single meaning in them. He contrasts the unfolding of Kafka's parables with the unfolding of other parables and compares this to the unfolding of a bud into a flower:

> The word "unfolding" has a double meaning. A bud unfolds into a blossom, but the boat which one teaches children to make by folding paper unfolds into a flat sheet of paper. This second kind of "unfolding" is really appropriate to the parable; it is the reader's pleasure to smooth it out so that he has the meaning on the palm of his hand. Kafka's parables, however, unfold in the first sense, the way a bud turns into a blossom.[41]

Other parables offer a meaning that one can grasp and hold "on the palm of [one's] hand"; the Kafkan parable offers no such easily accessible meaning. The reader of other parables is the agent of unfolding, the one who smooths out the complex folds of the parable into a simpler form. The Kafkan parable, by contrast, is the agent of its own unfolding. If one sought to unfold a blossom as one would unfold a paper boat, one would destroy it. The bud's self-unfolding constitutes a metamorphosis into a new form, with greater complexity not less, that cannot be reversed. Further, in its unfolding, the blossom, like the Kafkan parable, makes visible something that had previously been inaccessible.

Benjamin's two meanings of unfolding map onto two ways of interpreting texts: In the first, one unfolds the text into its meaning, as one unfolds a paper boat into a smooth piece of paper. The parable presents its meaning as an object to be discovered, and the reader takes pleasure in doing so. The form exists for the purpose of the process of unfolding. In the other meaning, one witnesses the unfolding of the text as one would witness the unfolding of a bud into a blossom; there is a pleasure, but it is not the pleasure of mastery. We cannot make the bud blossom; we are not the agents of its unfolding. Likewise, our relation with the Kafkan parable is not one of use or mastery or possession but one of receptivity and engagement. One engages the meaning, relationally, aesthetically, in an ongoing process, but one never captures it once and for all. The pleasure is in its perception, not its possession.[42] Thus, Benjamin suggests that Kafka's parables unfold in a manner different from other parables and that they must be interpreted in a different way. One cannot extract a meaning from them; according to Benjamin, they "are never exhausted by what is explainable."[43]

Walter Sokel's description of *The Trial*, that "the text resists the attempt at *unambiguous* understanding,"[44] is applicable to all of Kafka's work. But note that the resistance here is not obstinacy; there is more at stake. If something has multiple or changing meanings, then "*unambiguous* understanding" is not really understanding; it is interpretation as wish fulfillment. It is a claim to interpretation that requires the erasure of the ambiguity that is an integral part of what it is interpreting. It is a reductive interpretation, but it is also a reductive interpretation of interpretation itself. The inexhaustibility of meaning to which Benjamin points in Kafka's works requires a mode of interpretation that does not claim to have figured out the one true meaning but also does not disengage, in despair, from the effort to interpret. Life requires this same kind of interpretive activity. The truths of the world and the people in it are ever changing, never simple, and always just beyond our grasp, though not beyond our glimpse. We seek and find, but find only a portion of what we seek; we search but catch only a fleeting glance, and yet this partial finding is something, is perhaps the only something. This is not a grand view of interpretation and its possibilities; rather, it is a modest but realistic one given Kafka's view of the world.

In this book, I argue that Kafka's works are deeply engaged in interpretation and in finding a way of engaging the complexity of the world without falling prey to the two temptations that he depicts in his stories: the temptation to hermeneutical tyranny and the temptation to hermeneutical despair. The threat of violence, sheer destruction, is never far away, always remains as a present possibility; likewise, the possibility of not finding sustenance to stay alive is also always present. For Kafka, the process of interpretation can be subject to the violence of tyranny, on the one hand, or the despair of deprivation, on the other. In tyranny, interpretation becomes decipherment and definition; in despair, interpretation withers. In both, interpretation ceases, through claims of completion at one end of the spectrum and through an inability to engage in it at the other. Kafka is, I argue, a particularly skillful explorer of the terrain of interpretation, one who maps the sites of danger, characterized by tyranny and despair, and the sites where construction of some sort might be possible. In these latter sites, there is the possibility, however small and frail, of making some sort of connection with others and of finding a way of being at home in the world. There is also, I argue, a way of reading Kafka's ethics of interpretation.

Chapter 1

The Tyranny of Simplicity and the Fantasy of Completion

Kafka's "Letter to His Father" and Freud's *Interpretation of Dreams*

"Life is more than a . . . puzzle," Kafka states near the end of his now-famous letter to his father, written in November of 1919.[1] With a little patience and persistence, a puzzle can be pieced together and solved. Life, on the other hand, is more complex. There will always be something left over, something that does not quite fit, some "more than" that cannot be interpreted. Likewise, Kafka writes to his father, the problems in their relationship cannot be completely explained or solved, and Kafka describes his attempt to do so in the letter as an impossible task: "Naturally things cannot in reality fit together the way the evidence does in my letter" (125). Nevertheless, he claims, the effort to interpret their relationship is not futile: by writing the letter, "something has been achieved which so closely approximates the truth that it might reassure us both a little and make our living and our dying easier" (125). But what exactly has the letter accomplished? What is this approximation of the truth to which Kafka points?

In this chapter, I bring together Kafka's "Letter to His Father" with Sigmund Freud's *The Interpretation of Dreams* in order to think about the possibilities and limits of interpretation and the desires and drives active in it. Kafka's letter, I argue, describes two modes of interpretation while performing yet another, and in the interplay between these modes of interpretation, we begin to see his ethics of interpretation. I look briefly at two passages in *The Interpretation of Dreams* in which Freud oscillates between claiming to have completed interpretation of a dream, on the one hand, and declaring that it is impossible ever to completely interpret a dream, on the other. In a reversal of the usual pairing of Freud and

Kafka, in which Freud's theories of the unconscious or the Oedipal complex are used to unpack Kafka's texts and his relationship with his father, I use Kafka's hermeneutics to unpack the dynamics of a hermeneutical drive in Freud.

Freud uses a literary text—the story of Oedipus—to reveal the dynamics of the family drama, but here Kafka's family drama helps to reveal the dynamics of Freud's psychoanalytic text and his internal hermeneutical drama. The conflict between Kafka's own mode of interpretation and his father's mode are dramatized in Freud himself. Kafka's family drama enables us to better recognize Freud's internal drama, rather than Freud's presentation of the family drama enabling us to interpret Kafka's internal drama. This reversal aims to read better the tensions that exist in all of us engaged in interpretation—the tension between our fantasies of complete interpretation, closure, and mastery, on the one hand, and, on the other, our encounters with texts in which we learn interpretation as a form of engagement rather than mastery, dialogue rather than decipherment. Freud's own oscillations, read through the lens of Kafka's hermeneutics, illustrate the temptation each reader faces to abandon the complexity of a text by claiming to have completely interpreted it.

Kafka's ethics of interpretation points us toward interpretive activity that forgoes mastery for engagement; relinquishes the satisfactions of closure for the joys but also frustrations of ongoing dialogue; and seeks not completion but approximations, acknowledging that complete interpretation is itself a fantasy that obscures the glimpses we might be able to achieve.

Battling Modes of Interpretation

Kafka's contrast between a puzzle and life points to a contrast between two ways of interpreting—his own and his father's—that are also two modes of engaging the world. While his father finds the world readily amenable to his interpretations and easily solvable, Kafka sees the world as more complex and less easily explained. What is simple to his father is complicated to Kafka. What his father deems self-evident remains, at least in part, unfathomable to his son. Where his father declares a single, complete explanation, Kafka finds multiple, partial ones. What his father sees as unchanging truth shifts before Kafka's very eyes. These different conceptions of life and the world result in different modes of interpretation: while his father interprets things definitively and decisively with a sense of mastery, Kafka approaches them from multiple, conflicting viewpoints. For Kafka, the activity of interpretation is not a means of arriving at definitive interpretations but of navigating, and engaging with, the complexities and contingencies of the world around him. The most one can hope for is an approximation of the truth, not a complete interpretation.

In keeping with his sense of the complexity of things, Kafka presents three different, though interrelated, versions of his father in the course of the letter: tragic hero, failed parent, and hermeneutical tyrant. In Kafka's description of these different versions of his father, he also presents three different versions of himself. When he laments the fate of his father as a tragic hero, he is himself also a tragic hero, and the tragedy consists in their being paired as father and son despite incompatible personalities and temperaments. When he complains about the failures of his father as a parent, he depicts himself as the awestruck and fearful child, suffering his father's failings. Finally, in the scenes in which his father is portrayed as a hermeneutical tyrant, Kafka depicts himself as the impotent subject cowering in wait for the tyrant's pronouncement against him.

But there is also another father and another Kafka in the letter, as we shall see: the Kafka who writes the letter and the father who speaks near the end of it. As writer, Kafka is no longer the tragically fated character, the unfairly treated son, or the cowering subject; instead, he is the creator of worlds in which the complexities of life, the shifting nature of things, the contingencies of what happens, and the incomplete nature of what we are able to grasp are put before our eyes. This kind of world, and the writing that produces it, is not amenable to the interpretational mode of the hermeneutical tyrant—one that seeks to define and master—but rather calls its readers to a different mode of reading and of engagement, one that relinquishes the expectation of a single, determinate meaning, that allows for the living and changing nature of what we call truth,[2] and that forgoes the temptation of complete interpretation and seeks instead approximations of the truth.

Kafka's "Letter to His Father" is both about and to his father, but it is also a piece of writing that in its very form resists the father's mode of interpretation and calls for the father (and, by extension, Kafka's readers) to interpret in a new way, one more akin to Kafka's own—one that sees the complexity of their relationship, the plurality of perspectives that might be taken on it, and the shifting nature of it over time. In paying attention to what the letter performs, alongside what it explicitly states, we begin to see the outlines of Kafka's ethics of interpretation.

The Letter's Opening

A document of more than one hundred handwritten pages, Kafka's "Letter to His Father" begins with an emphasis on complexity.[3] The careful structuring of the first paragraph is reminiscent of a puzzle in its multiple elements, but Kafka puts the emphasis on his inability to fit all the pieces neatly together and solve the puzzle. He begins by stating, "You asked me recently why I maintain that I am afraid of you" (7).[4] His father does not ask Kafka why he *is* afraid of him, but rather why he *maintains* (*behaupte*) that he is afraid of him. The question carries the undercurrent of an accusation, the suggestion that Kafka maintains that he is afraid of his father without actually being so and does so for some suspect reason that his father would like to find out.

Like his father's wording of the question, Kafka's wording of the letter's opening is also worth noting. Rather than beginning with a statement such as "in this letter, I will explain the reasons for my fear of you . . ." or "I write to respond to your recent question," Kafka begins with the word *Du* and with his father's actions: his father's asking the question. By doing so, Kafka emphasizes that his father is, in one sense, the instigator of the letter. The suggestion, which is a blueprint for one of the main arguments of the letter, is that Kafka's action (in this case, writing the letter) is a response to his father's action, rather than one taken out of his own free agency, and consequently not something for which he can be held solely responsible.

The first sentence reads like a carefully worded opening statement by a defense lawyer in a trial, stating the accusation made and then going on to respond to the accusation. Kafka gives two reasons for his inability to answer his father's question, noting that each is only a partial reason.[5] The first is simply the *fact* that he is afraid of his father: because he is afraid of him, he finds it difficult to talk and think, as well as to answer questions, in his father's presence. The second is the complexity of the grounds for his fear: there are "far more details than I could even approximately keep in mind while talking" (7). These two reasons make it impossible for him to give any answer in conversation with his father; they also make him unable to give a *complete* answer in the letter: "Even in writing, this fear and its consequences hamper me in relation to you and because the magnitude of the subject matter goes far beyond the scope of my memory and power of reasoning" (7). Note that Kafka registers the complexity of the situation to his own cognitive abilities: there are more details than he can hold together; the material goes beyond his memory and understanding. Because of both his fear and his inability to hold together, remember, and understand the complexity of the situation, the answer given in the letter will, he writes, "still be very incomplete" (7).

In contrast to the complexity Kafka sees in the situation, to his father "the matter always seemed very simple" (7). The opening paragraph encapsulates the contrast between Kafka's view and his father's: the former sees the complexity in things, sees the possibility only for partial answers, finds that things exceed his capacities for understanding; the latter sees things simply and clearly and completely. Even the statement "I am afraid of you" is read in radically different ways by father and son. According to his father, the interpretation is simple: the statement is false, a self-serving lie on Kafka's part. According to Kafka, the reality to which the statement refers is complex, and the complexity of the reasons for his fears, and the fear itself, make it impossible to explain it adequately.

Two versions of the father-son relationship are in confrontation here, and a crucial issue in each is the question of guilt. Who is to blame for the situation in which Kafka and his father find themselves? According to the letter, Kafka's father places all the blame on his son and none on himself. From his point of view, his son's claim to be afraid of him is really just an excuse for his "coldness, estrangement, and ingratitude" (9), and his hiding in his room has more to do with a lack of sympathy than an excess of fear. His son seeks to gain at his father's expense, all while narrating their relationship as the false story of his own oppression. In short, Kafka's father sees himself as completely blameless, even as the true victim in their relationship.

Things are not so clear-cut for Kafka. Kafka sees a multiplicity of reasons—each of which offers only a partial explanation and changes over time—for the problems in his relationship with his father. He depicts their relationship in three different, though interrelated, ways; these three intertwined strands each suggest a different way that the letter can be read—as the telling of a tragedy, as the complaints of a son, or as the presentation of the prosecution's case in a legal trial. Kafka moves from lamenting the tragic fate of a mismatched father and son to complaining about his father's failings as a parent and finally to prosecuting a hermeneutical tyrant. These are three different narratives with different characters, but the same two actors, Kafka and his father, appear in each.

The Tragic Pairing

Kafka's letter to his father can be read as a lament written from the perspective of an adult looking back on his childhood with the more objective judgment of age and maturity: "The child's exclusive sense of guilt has been partly replaced by insight into our helplessness, yours and mine" (33). He writes about the tragic circumstances preventing father and son from mutual understanding and affection; they are fellow sufferers in an unfortunate fate. Walter Sokel highlights the way in which this tragic framework dispenses with guilt but not condemnation: "Kafka absolves his father of all intentional guilt and malice, but instead invokes an inexorable necessity, a tragic fate, condemning both himself and his father to interminable sufferings from and through each other."[6] They are "victims," and neither is to be viewed as the guilty party. Kafka tells his father, "The effect you had on me was the effect you could not help having" (15).

Whatever harm his father caused Kafka was not his father's fault but rather the result of this tragic pairing. For example, his father's well-intentioned attempts to teach him to swim became for Kafka lessons in "profound humiliation" (19), so big and strong was his father and so weak and small did he perceive himself to be in comparison. As a child, he was unable to think things through, reflect on them, and see them in perspective. In writing the letter, he distinguishes between his emotional responses to events at the time as a child and his reflections on them as an adult, acknowledging that he writes mainly not "of the child's reflections, but of his feelings" (29). The multiplying of roles and perspectives increases here with the addition of a diachronic axis of child and adult.

This tragedy is caused in part by their inherited family traits and the unfortunate hand fate dealt them in putting them together as father and son. Kafka describes himself as "a Löwy [his mother's family name] with a certain basis of Kafka, which, however, is not set in motion by the Kafka will to life, business, and conquest, but by a Löwyish spur that impels more secretly, more diffidently, and in another direction, and which often fails to work entirely" (11). His father, in contrast, is "a true Kafka in strength, health, appetite, loudness of voice, eloquence, self-satisfaction, worldly dominance, endurance, presence of mind, knowledge of human nature, a certain way of doing things on a grand scale" (13). In any other relationship, Kafka argues, they could have gotten along quite well: "I should have been happy to have you as a friend, as a boss, an uncle, a grandfather, even (though rather more hesitantly) as a father-in-law" (11). However, as "a true Kafka" and an odd Kafka-Löwy mix, they are tragically incompatible in the roles of father and son.

No one is to blame for their estrangement, according to this reading. Any fault of father and son is like the fault of the tragic hero, who incurs punishment through his tragic flaw rather than through any intentional wrongdoing. The agency of guilt is made ambiguous, such that it is impossible to distinguish between guilt and fate in much the same way that, as Kafka argues, "'doing' and 'happening' cannot be kept clearly distinct" (101). Agency, and thus also guilt, is obscured here. Weakness is Kafka's tragic flaw; strength is his father's. The father's strength cannot help but damage the son in his weakness. Neither is guilty, though both play an assigned part in this tragic drama. Read in this way, the letter mourns their unfortunate fate and presents a compelling argument for why Kafka's father should see them both as equally guiltless. Though adulthood allows Kafka to see their conflict as a tragedy of fate, this perspective offers no means of rectifying the situation, for the problem stems from their natures—natures they cannot change. They must both simply accept their fate and not blame themselves or each other.

The Father's Failings

The tragic reading of the relationship between Kafka and his father is only one strand in a multistranded hermeneutic effort on Kafka's part. Beneath the surface of Kafka's claim of finding his father guiltless are stinging details that outline his father's failings as a parent. The tragically mismatched pair of the previous reading, pushed together by cruel fate, becomes a thoughtless, self-centered father and his long-suffering son. Kafka details wrongs he endured as a child—and, to some extent, still endures—and points out his father's character flaws, errors of judgment, and failings in parenting, all the while still claiming that he considers his father blameless. However, the sheer quantity and detail of things for which Kafka criticizes his father in the letter suggest that even if the peculiar perspective of the child is taken into account, the father is certainly not blameless.

While ostensibly arguing for the innocence of both himself and his father, Kafka gives a detailed account of his father's faults and failures. For example, Kafka criticizes his father for not following the rules he himself set. At the dinner table, all food was to be eaten without comment on its taste, bones were not to be cracked, and no crumbs dropped. The only activity allowed at the table, the rule went, was eating. However, his father broke all these rules: "You, so tremendously the authoritative man, did not keep up the commandments you imposed on me" (27–29).

In addition to failing to keep his own rules, the father is charged with having no thought or concern for how his words affect others. Recalling his father's response to one of his friends, Kafka declares, "Without knowing him you compared him, in some dreadful way that I have now forgotten, to vermin" (25).[7] Whenever Kafka took an interest in someone, his father was ready "without any consideration for [Kafka's] feelings or respect for [his] judgment, to move in with abuse, defamation, and denigration" (25). Kafka criticizes his father for being self-centered, unable to see things from anyone else's perspective or take an interest in anything other than himself: "Even today you really only encourage me in anything when you yourself are involved in it, when what is at stake is your own sense of self-importance" (19). All revolves around his father.

Kafka's main complaint is that his father holds him completely responsible for all that is wrong in their relationship; in contrast, he claims to consider his father guiltless. And yet these claims not to blame his father often come just before or just after he has explicitly criticized his father or recounted some action of his father's to which blame would be a natural reaction. Peter Mailloux compares part of the letter to "a series of guerilla attacks."[8] For example, Kafka describes his father paradoxically as a blameless tormentor: "Nor was it at all a good contribution to the children's upbringing the way you—of course, without being in the slightest to blame for it yourself—tormented her on our account" (61). Here Kafka criticizes his father's treatment of Kafka's mother and the effect that had on Kafka and his siblings while simultaneously claiming that his father is not "in the slightest to blame" for that.

Rhetorically the insertion of "without being in the slightest to blame for it yourself" in the middle of the sentence undercuts the father's ability to defend himself. By claiming that his complaints are merely a means of self-defense—"again, by no means a reproach, but only a refutation of your reproaches" (83)—Kafka undercuts his father's ability to defend himself against them. The father is being accused, but since the accuser denies he is casting any blame, the one accused is left with little means to protest.

Further, Kafka traces all his own failings back to his father, such that the father's reproaches function like boomerangs bringing the blame back onto his own shoulders. The letter gives ample evidence for seeing the father as responsible for instilling a sense of fear in his son, the fear that led, Kafka states, to his inability to think, speak, or remember certain details in his father's presence. This fear of his father also shadows him when he is writing, and thus even away from his father's physical presence Kafka is unable to escape completely from his influence.

When Kafka engages in self-reproaches, they merely add fuel to the fire of his reproach of his father, since everything he thinks about himself derives from his father's influence: "As I now am, I am (apart, of course, from the fundamentals and the influence of life itself) the result of your upbringing and of my obedience" (33). When Kafka confesses, "I lazed away more time on the sofa than you in all your life, including all your illnesses" (91), or declares, "Something like my cold indifference, scarcely disguised, indestructible, childishly helpless, approaching the ridiculous, and brutishly complacent, the indifference of a self-sufficient but coldly imaginative child, I have never found anywhere else" (89), he is describing what his father's methods of upbringing, and his obedience to them, have created. No matter how severe his self-reproaches, they always end up as even more severe reproaches of his father: "This sense of nothingness that often dominates me . . . comes largely from your influence" (17). By tracing his own faults back to his father's influence or actions, Kafka co-opts the vehemence of his father's reproaches to fuel his own reproaches of his father, but he does so under the veil of merely defending himself. In other words, the father's power is turned back against him, thereby strengthening the son's reproach.

In this reading of the letter, it seems that Kafka wants his father to recognize his own failings and stop blaming his son for everything. This is not about a tragic fate but about bad parenting. The more Kafka reproaches himself, the more he thereby reproaches his father even more severely. This amounts to Kafka's blaming everything on his father, which mirrors his father's blaming everything on his son. The difference is that while his father issues his reproaches as direct attacks, Kafka takes a circuitous and subversive route. The reason for this is the power differential between them. As we shall see in the next section, Kafka has recourse only to this sort of attack because the supreme power of his father as the hermeneutical tyrant precludes direct attacks on Kafka's part.

The Hermeneutical Tyrant

Kafka does more in the letter than simply point out the ways his father failed as a parent: he undertakes something akin to a legal prosecution. His father is charged with being not merely a domineering father but also a hermeneutical tyrant. Heinz Politzer identifies the constellation of words that evoke the image of the hermeneutical tyrant: "The letter bristles with epithets like 'superior,' 'sovereign,' 'despotic,' and 'tyrannical.' "[9] His father is guilty not just of bad parenting but also of claiming complete hermeneutical power, of hermeneutical tyranny, of viewing his own interpretations as the only right ones and all others as irrelevant or false. Stach declares, "It was the portrait of a domestic tyrant."[10] Kafka writes,

> You had unbounded confidence in your opinion. That was not yet so dazzling for me as a child as later for the boy growing up. From your armchair you ruled the world. Your opinion was correct, every other was mad, wild, *meshugge*, not normal. Your self-confidence indeed was so great that you had no need to be consistent at all and yet never ceased to be in the right. (21)

His father eclipses the space between his interpretation and "the truth"; his interpretation *is* the truth, or rather, the truth is created by his interpretation. He does not need to fulfill some sort of criterion, such as accuracy, consistency, or truthfulness, by which others might judge his interpretations as convincing or accurate. His interpretation rules not because it is the most accurate or reasonable one but because it is *his* interpretation: "For me you took on the enigmatic quality that all tyrants have whose rights are based on their person and not on reason" (21).

Kafka portrays his father as the omnipotent interpreter, one who has the power to interpret everything and everyone in the world. Frederick J. Hoffman highlights the relation between the father's authority and his power to impose his interpretation as the only legitimate one: "The father becomes a tyrant; his authority is unquestioned. . . . Protests against it on grounds of reason or justice only aggravate the wound; for reasonable protest does not avail against the tyranny."[11] In the face of such power, Kafka's fear prevents him from speaking; he is unable to defend himself against his father's accusations. Max Brod points to the father's overwhelming power: "In the 'Letter' his father's verdict is given a wholly disproportionate power of deciding the life or death of all of Kafka's efforts."[12] His father rejects all interpretations other than his own "not only selectively but in every respect, and finally nobody [is] left except [himself]" (21). There is no space for multiple perspectives, complexities, subtleties, mysteries, or contingencies.

Kafka's sense of the complexity and magnitude of why he is afraid of his father is connected to his sense of his father's magnitude and the extent of his reach. Kafka imagines him stretched across a map of the world; only the outermost regions are untouched by his body. And it is only in those outermost regions where Kafka can find some escape from his father's influence: "Sometimes I imagine the map of the world spread out and you stretched diagonally across it. And I feel as if I could consider living in only those regions that either are not covered by you or are not within your reach" (115). In his father's presence, he is unable to formulate or voice any opinion that conflicts with his father's; in fact, he tells his father, he is unable even to think or speak in that context.[13] Even responding to his father's questions proves difficult, a fact to which the letter itself testifies. Linguistic competence dissolves into the passivity of listening in his father's presence.

In contrast to the "unbounded confidence" of his father, Kafka describes himself as having "lost confidence in [his] own actions" and as "wavering, doubtful" (37); his mistrust of others becomes "mistrust of [himself] and perpetual anxiety about everything else" (75). Kafka's hermeneutical incapacity does not arise, he argues, from faulty logic, imprecise comprehension, or inconsistency. In his father's realm, the attributes of rationality, accuracy, and consistency are neither important nor necessary for hermeneutical supremacy. The power of an interpretation in that realm arises from the authority of the person rather than any inherent value in the interpretation itself, and in this authority, Kafka is lacking. While his father needs no reassurance from others, Kafka views his father's opinion of him as supremely important: "My valuation of myself was much more dependent on you than on anything else, such as some external success" (93). Kafka's father is the interpretive authority and as such he functions as a hermeneutical tyrant. Even in the letter itself, Kafka seeks his father's recognition of the validity of his view of the relationship. Politzer draws a connection between the Kafka described in the letter—what I would call the character of Kafka the son—and other Kafkan characters: "Reading the letter, one cannot escape the feeling that Kafka, like his protagonist Georg Bendemann, would have thrown himself from a bridge had his father so ordained."[14] Given his father's hermeneutical tyranny, Kafka faces three options: submission, flight, or fight. For Kafka, submission would mean the dissolution of his very self given his father's omnipotence and view of his son. Fight seems to be an impossible goal, so sure is defeat the outcome. Flight seems to be the only possible means of survival.

Growing up, Kafka looked for avenues of flight: "I fled everything that even remotely reminded me of you" (53). His attempts at escape took different forms, but all turned out to be failures. Marriage seemed the most likely means of escape—it might, Kafka thought, have ushered in a sense of equality between father and son—but Kafka was unable to successfully pursue this avenue. Kafka describes his movements toward marriage as "the most grandiose and hopeful attempts at escape" (97), but consequently his inability to carry through with any of his engagements constituted "correspondingly grandiose" (97) failures. In a world dominated by his father, escape seems almost impossible. Referring to the regions in which he might escape his father's influence, Kafka writes, "In keeping with the conception I have of your magnitude, these [regions] are not many and not very comforting regions—and marriage is not among them" (115). Kafka gives multiple reasons for why he has ruled out marriage. It turns out to be part of his father's "territory" and thus unavailable to him. In addition, Kafka's anxieties about himself and his fear that he has none of the qualities necessary for the role of a "good family man" make his attempts at marriage falter. But above all, his fear that marriage might hinder his writing necessitates renouncing it as an option. It is only writing that offers a real possibility of escape.

Writing as Escape

From the beginning of the letter, Kafka sets up a topography of power: there is the realm of conversation, in which his father is all-powerful and Kafka is unable to speak, and there is the realm of writing, where Kafka gains a voice, though one still hampered by fear and incapacity. Despite these limitations, it is the realm of writing that, for Kafka, holds the only hope. With writing he is able to get "some distance away from [his father] by [his] own efforts" (85), find some relief from the weight of his father's influence, and gain "a chance to breathe freely" (87).

For example, it is only by writing the letter that Kafka is able to respond to his father's question about why he is afraid of him. Sokel argues that writing "was the region to which the son could flee and which he cultivated because it was the one area in the world where his father's powerful influence did not extend. Speech was linked to the father's forbidding and threatening presence, but writing dealt with his absence."[15] This absence is reinforced by his father's lack of interest in his writing:

> The aversion you naturally and immediately took to my writing was, for once, welcome to me. My vanity, my ambition did suffer under your soon proverbial way of hailing the arrival of my books: "Put it on my bedside table!" . . . but I was really quite glad of it, not only out of rebellious malice, not only out of delight at a new confirmation of my view of our relationship, but quite spontaneously, because to me that formula sounded something like: "Now you are free!" (87)

His father's lack of interest moves writing into one of those regions on the map beyond his father's reach—or seems to do so. And yet, even in this passage, we see Kafka's reliance on his father as the authority. The father's declaration "Put it on my bedside table!" becomes a "new confirmation of [Kafka's] view of [their] relationship"—one that brings him "delight," as if Kafka's view requires these instances of confirmation from his father. The father's declaration also becomes in Kafka's ears a pronouncement of freedom, with the ring of permission given. Kafka is not taking leave of his father in this passage so much as he is being given permission to do so.

For though through writing Kafka creates a realm in which he can speak away from his father's presence, escape proves a hope yet to be realized rather than a goal attained: "Of course it was a delusion; I was not, or, to put it most optimistically, was not yet, free" (87). For Kafka tells his father: "My writing was about you; I only lamented there what I could not lament upon your breast."[16] In this short sentence, Kafka gives us a remarkably multivalent description of his writing, particularly when we focus on what he means by "my writing" and by "lament." In German as in English, "my writing" (*mein Schreiben*) can mean both the act of writing and what it produces. Kafka states that he engages in the activity of writing because he cannot speak to his father: the act of writing substitutes for the intimacy and physicality of the child leaning against his father's chest, talking to him.[17] Kafka's pen serves as a substitute for his voice speaking to his father; the page of paper serves as a substitute for his father's ear.

But Kafka also declares that his writing—that is, the pieces of writing that are produced by the activity of putting pen to paper—is what he would have said to his father if their relationship had been better. This is a striking description of his stories, which are rather unlike what one might imagine a son saying while "lamenting" on his father's chest! His writing, he declares, is what he would have said both *to* his father and *about* his father: "My writing was about you." His stories are filled with figures who bear a striking resemblance to Hermann Kafka, most notably Georg Bendemann's father in "The Judgment" and Gregor Samsa's father in "The Metamorphosis." Kafka wrote the letter several years after he wrote these stories, but the father he describes in the letter clearly serves as a model for these fathers. Further, Kafka's statement that his writing is about his father refers to deeper dynamics than just his father serving as a role model for certain characters. For Kafka, his father represents a fundamental way of interpreting the world, one characterized by confidence yet inconsistency, singularity and simplicity, and an unwillingness to look at dissenting views or simply any other views. It is a mode of interpretation that Kafka both despises and admires, and it is the mode of interpretation that his father uses and that authority figures utilize in their dealings with the Kafkan protagonist.

Kafka's statement that his writing was about his father can mean, first, that the act of writing substitutes for the act of speaking with his father; second, that what he writes is what he would have said to his father in person if their relationship were different; and third, that what he writes about—that is, the subject matter of that writing—is about his father. Writing is hardly an escape from his father.

Like the multivalence of the term "my writing," the verb *klagen*, translated as "lament," also has a striking range of meanings in German. Kafka's statement "Ich klagte dort ja nur, was ich an Deiner Brust nicht klagen konnte" (I only lamented there what I could not lament upon your breast) can be translated in different ways. The verb *klagen* can mean to lament, complain, or make a legal complaint, among other things. These three meanings of the verb map onto the three ways in which Kafka describes his father: he *laments* the fate of the tragic heroes (including himself in that category); he *complains* about the failings of his father as a bad parent; and he *makes a legal complaint*, a charge of criminality or worse against the hermeneutical tyrant. His writing is a form of lament, complaint, and prosecution. But in all three, the energy is focused on his father. In writing, Kafka gains enough distance to regain his voice, but hardly enough distance to be free of his father.

Writing as Attack

The description of Kafka's writing as prosecution is important to keep in mind when reading the conclusion of the letter and thinking about what the letter as a piece of writing performs. For while Kafka describes his writing as a form of escape and a "long-drawn-out leave-taking" (87) from his father, the writing that the letter itself constitutes takes the form of a prosecution. Kafka describes it to Milena as "a lawyer's letter" and tells her to look for all the lawyer's tricks in it.[18] The statement that "things cannot in reality fit together the way the evidence does in my letter" (125) implies that he has carefully, even artfully, fit together the evidence in the letter. Kafka develops the case against his father with careful attention to the argument's narrative structure, its rhetorical power, and its dramatic effect. John Urzidil describes the letter as "an indictment of the tyrannical Father-God, an attempt at analysis, both militant and humble, of the fundamental conflicts between the two worlds of father and son."[19] The odd combination, "militant and humble," suggests the complex nature of these "fundamental conflicts," which include their tragic pairing but also their battle of interpretation. This battle, present even in the very first sentence of the letter, involves both whose interpretation of their relationship will win out and whose mode of interpretation will prove the stronger.

Although Kafka claims throughout the letter not to be blaming his father, the letter builds like a prosecution, lining up the evidence against the father. Each version of the father suggests a different level of guilt, increasing as the roles develop: the tragic hero is blameless for any intentional wrongdoing and the parent is guilty only of his specific failings as a father, but the hermeneutical tyrant is ontologically guilty on a cosmic scale.

In the letter, Kafka seeks his father's recognition of his (Kafka's) interpretation of their relationship—not as the only interpretation but as one with as much validity as his father's view of it. However, the father's compliance with such a request would be a radical overturning of his own hermeneutical mode—hermeneutical tyranny. For while Kafka argues for the possibility of multiple perspectives and interpretations—"what is innocence in you may be guilt in me, and vice versa" (101)—his father insists on one perspective and one interpretation—his own. Were he to acknowledge Kafka's proposed view that they are both guiltless, he would be transgressing his own hermeneutical principles.

It is as the writer of the letter that we begin to see a different Kafka—not the tragic hero ill-fated to be matched with such a father, not the fearful son brought up by a bad father, and not the impotent subject cowering before the hermeneutical tyrant. Instead what emerges in the performance of the letter is Kafka the writer with the power to speak and to prosecute the hermeneutical tyrant, or at least argue a case against him. His father is blameless as the tragic hero and merely reproached as a failing parent, but the charge of hermeneutical tyranny places the guilt firmly on the father's shoulders. Kafka charges his father with having a "mania for domination" (57) and an "imperious temperament" (31); engaging in "not only cursing, but other sorts of tyrannizing" (55); being a "giant" (41), an "autocrat" (71), and an "all-important personage" (23). He even connects his father with infernal horrors in remembering that his father's "gurgling laughter . . . gave the child its first notion of hell" (41). No sympathy is expressed; no truce is sought. Frederick R. Karl argues that in the letter "Kafka's attack presupposes . . . a verdict already delivered. Only here he is the prosecuting attorney; for the first time, Kafka the lawyer is not on trial."[20] While posing, at the opening of the letter, as a defense lawyer representing himself and responding to his father's accusations, Kafka becomes the prosecuting attorney. It is the judge himself, Kafka's father, who becomes the one accused.

The Father's Rejoinder

The letter concludes with two sections. First, Kafka offers a rejoinder to what he has written so far in the letter but does so in his father's voice. He leads into the section with the following: "If you look at the reasons I offer for the fear I have of you, you might answer" (121). Then, in the final paragraph of the letter, he responds to the rejoinder in his own voice. Looking at each section in turn proves crucial to understanding the ways in which Kafka is presenting an alternative hermeneutical mode to that of his father.

Both the content of the father's rejoinder and the role that it performs in the letter are important, for Kafka highlights the rejoinder as being the part of the letter that accomplishes something of note. The father's opening statement, "You maintain I make things easy for myself by explaining my relation to you as simply being your fault" (121),[21] echoes the letter's opening sentence, "You asked me recently why I maintain that I am afraid of you," by repeating the verb "maintain" (*behaupten*) and its implication of suspicion about Kafka's claims. The father does not refute the charge that he places the full blame for the state of their relationship on Kafka; rather, he shifts attention to the manner in which they each place blame on the other. The father says he does so frankly, but that his son does so without taking responsibility for the blame he places on his father. Instead, says the father of the rejoinder, his son claims that he himself is innocent and his father guilty, but that he will generously consider him to be not guilty, or, in the father's words, "that out of sheer magnanimity you are ready not only to forgive me but (what is both more and less) also to prove and be willing to believe yourself—contrary to the truth—that I also am not guilty" (123).

In keeping with his hermeneutical mode of deeming everything simple and easily explained, the father of the rejoinder takes the complexity and multiple strands of Kafka's presentation of their relationship and distills them into an even stronger charge of parasitism against Kafka, adding the judgment that Kafka is "unfit for life" (123). Just as Kafka increases the volume of blame as he moves from lament to complaint to prosecution over the course of the letter, so, too, does his father increase the volume of his blame:

> Basically, however, in this as in everything else you have only proved to me that all my reproaches were justified, and that one especially justified charge was still missing: namely, the charge of insincerity, obsequiousness, and parasitism. If I am not very much mistaken, you are preying on me even with this letter itself. (125)[22]

The father of the rejoinder gives no ground. He says that he fights fairly and frankly, but that his son fights like vermin, which "not only sting, but, on top of it, suck your blood in order to sustain their own life" (123). Not only is Kafka unfit for life but also, instead of taking responsibility for his own unfitness, he blames it on his father, so that he can "calmly stretch out and let [himself] be hauled through life, physically and mentally" (123), by his father. The father's rejoinder suggests that the letter has not cleared up anything nor brought any measure of reconciliation. In fact, it has revealed the need for even further charges against his son.

In the rejoinder, the father displays the tyrannical hermeneutics the letter has described him as engaging in. He finds nothing in the letter that in any way changes his own views; all evidence merely justifies and strengthens his view. Rather than opening up the father's interpretation of the relationship to the possibility of another view, the letter solidifies his sense of his own interpretation of their relationship as the right and only one. All other views are merely parasitic efforts, on his son's part, to prey on him. Complexity is mere obfuscation; the multiple other views are lies.

Kafka's Response

The father of the rejoinder is, of course, not really Kafka's father speaking but Kafka himself taking on his voice. As such, the father of the rejoinder is just as much a character as the fathers in Kafka's fiction, with whom he shares numerous attributes. Kafka explicitly identifies the constructed nature of the father's voice in his response to the rejoinder when he writes: "My answer to this is that, after all, this whole rejoinder—which can partly also be turned against you—does not come from you, but from me" (125). Why does Kafka include the rejoinder and then highlight that it is not really his father speaking but he himself?

Some critics read the rejoinder as a proleptic move in which Kafka anticipates the response of his father and lays it out ahead of time in order to refute it. Clayton Koelb describes the rhetorical movement of prolepsis as "anticipating one's interlocutor's discourse in such a way as to divest it of power. . . . Prolepsis provides a way of engaging in an intimate dialogue with a person who is in fact not present at all; the writer simply projects the addressee as a fictional voice within his own discourse."[23] Reading the rejoinder as proleptic suggests that Kafka is anticipating what his father might say in response to the letter in order to refute it. The prolepsis would function as a means of battle against his father. But does Kafka divest his father of power in the rejoinder?

On the one hand, the father of the rejoinder, by ignoring the numerous and complicated details of the letter, simply declaring his son unfit for life, and charging him with insincerity, obsequiousness, and parasitism, plays the role of the hermeneutical tyrant that Kafka has charged him with being. The father utters a condemnation of his son far more severe than any so far recounted in the bulk of the letter, and in doing so, he enacts and confirms Kafka's interpretation of him.

Further, the father of the rejoinder's condemnations of Kafka become, in the end, further condemnations of himself, since Kafka traces his failings back to his father's influence. The more vehement the father's charge against his son, the more vehement the charge against himself. When Kafka tells his father, "Not even your mistrust of others is as great as my self-mistrust, which you have bred in me" (125), he both one-ups his father's accusations against him (my mistrust of myself is greater than your mistrust of me) and puts the blame for that mistrust back on his father (you have bred this self-mistrust in me and, therefore, are to blame for it). Consequently, his father looks just as bad, or worse, after the rejoinder.

On the other hand, it would seem odd to suggest that the rejoinder divests the father of power, since the father of the rejoinder deflates the whole thrust of the letter by charging that in it Kafka is actually preying on him rather than offering his honest view of the relationship, a charge that causes one to reread the letter with just such a suspicion in mind and to find evidence to support such a charge. Kafka looks worse after the rejoinder, not better.

In addition, Kafka does not respond to the points raised in the rejoinder, much less refute them. He provides no explicit defense against the charge that he is preying on his father through the letter. Rather, he seems to praise the rejoinder above the rest of the letter, identifying the correction made by the rejoinder as the part of the letter that has accomplished something and thereby suggesting that there is some merit in the charge uttered against him in it. Therefore, the rejoinder hardly seems to divest the father of power or to create a straw man to destroy.

Neither reading—that the rejoinder shows the truth of Kafka's claims against his father or that it shows Kafka to be a parasitic son creating a false version of his father in order to prey on him—wins out. Both remain in play, even though they seem to be mutually exclusive. Jill Robbins identifies such a situation as a "paratactic juxtaposition of mutually exclusive claims" and connects it with Freud's discussion of jokes.[24] Neither reading can account fully for the meaning of the rejoinder, just as Kafka's reasons for his fear of his father can only, always, be partial answers.

Kafka's rejoinder keeps open the hermeneutical space, preventing its closure by a single interpretation, even his own, that claims to be authoritative. In this, the rejoinder and Kafka's response to it enact his hermeneutics of multiplicity, approximation, and contingency.

The fact that neither Kafka nor his father comes out as the clear winner after the rejoinder raises the question of just what the purpose of the rejoinder might be. Charles Bernheimer makes an observant comment about the role of authorities—extensions of the fictional fathers—in Kafka's fictional works: "The struggles of Joseph K. in *The Trial* and K. in *The Castle* are not battles against overwhelming paternal authorities but rather efforts to construct such authorities so that confrontation and battle can take place."[25] In the rejoinder, Kafka constructs the voice of his father and puts words in his mouth to create a confrontation that he is unable to have in person. Kafka as writer can move the conversation in whatever direction he wants—in contrast to the voiceless son fearfully facing his father in conversation. In writing, he co-opts his father's voice and speaks it, whereas in conversation his father's voice silences him. By giving voice to his father, Kafka creates a character with whom he can do battle. Koelb suggests that "the conversion of intractable persons into more readily manipulable texts is part of Kafka's strategy for dealing with both himself and others."[26] In writing the letter, Kafka attempts to reverse roles with his father: Kafka becomes the writer who speaks hoping to render his father the reader who "listens." Writing the letter therefore functions both as a flight from his father's physical presence and as a means of confronting him. He counters his father's tyrannical hermeneutics with his own hermeneutics to offer multiple interpretations of their relationship in a way that resists the tyranny of the father's one interpretation.

The vehemence and confidence of the father's voice in the rejoinder contrast with Kafka's tentative sense of a small accomplishment at the end of the letter. The end of the letter sounds a note not of triumph but of melancholy resignation, on the one hand, of hope for comfort, on the other. Kafka writes, "With the correction made by this rejoinder . . . in my opinion something has been achieved which so closely approximates the truth that it might reassure us both a little and make our living and our dying easier" (125). The achievement is no final victory, no complete interpretation of their relationship that settles things once and for all; it is only a close *approximation* of truth. Kafka frames this as merely his *opinion*—not the definitive statement on what the letter does or does not accomplish. And there is no *guarantee* that this will bring comfort, only that it *might* reassure both father and son, *might* make their living and dying easier. The possible accomplishment is a fragile one, but still *something.*

In this ending to the letter, Kafka forgoes the claim to have shown the final truth of their relationship, to have arrived at a complete interpretation or fully explained it, to have deciphered it once and for all. It is a hermeneutics of approximation that seeks to present multiple views as a means to battle hermeneutical tyranny. It is crucial not to overlook the fact that the claim to have approximated truth is a key element of battle against his father's hermeneutical tyranny. The modesty of Kafka's claim to have only approximated the truth is the means by which he wages an intense battle against hermeneutical tyranny—a subversive battle that must choose different weapons to make any headway. The battle against hermeneutical tyranny is waged by the very fragility of the achievement in relation to truth. Though the claim is modest, its function is powerful. Were the father to accept that only an approximation of truth is possible in the interpretation of their relationship, he would thereby lose the battle and relinquish his role as hermeneutical tyrant. For his part, Kafka's subversive hermeneutics is costly as it seeks to divest tyranny of its power through its own resisting of the temptation to step into the tyrant's place. As we shall see in the next two chapters, Georg Bendemann and Gregor Samsa attempt similar moves but can do so only at the very end of their lives . . . and at the cost of their own lives.

Keeping in mind the contrasting hermeneutics of father and son, I now turn to Kafka's contemporary, Sigmund Freud, to engage his struggle between these two modes of interpretation—a tyranny that claims the power of complete interpretation and the subversion of that power through the recognition of its limits—and explore the ways in which the father's mode of interpretation, hermeneutical tyranny, exists as a temptation for all of us. Reiner Stach draws a close connection between Freud and Kafka's "Letter to His Father" when he writes,

> Kafka's "Letter to His Father" is an indisputably powerful analysis of bourgeois psychogenesis, in particular of the psychological roots of power and dependence. Kafka's letter is on par with Freud's case studies in its vividness, clarity, and intuitive grasp of the exemplary, the perceptual power of which extends far beyond the individual. It is obvious that psychoanalytical literature influenced the letter, but Kafka never relies on general hypotheses or gives in to the temptation to curtail strenuous arguments with psychological constructs and terminology. He was at the height of his intellectual and linguistic powers, and his letter, read as autobiographical testimony, is one of the most impressive that has ever been published.[27]

Freud and the Fantasy of Complete Interpretation

Recalling Kafka's statement that "life is more than a puzzle; the pieces cannot all fit together as the evidence does in this letter," it is perhaps surprising that we read in Freud of a similar recognition of this "more than" quality of things, since he is so frequently charged with reducing everything to a puzzle that can be solved—and often to one particular Oedipal puzzle. Pericles Lewis contrasts Freud's mode of interpretation with Kafka's, suggesting drastic discontinuities between them: "Freud's an aggressive probing of appearances to find a hidden truth, Kafka's a melancholy but inconclusive speculation."[28] Susan Sontag adds to the characterizing of Freud's hermeneutics as aggressive:

> The most celebrated and influential doctrines, those of Marx and Freud, actually amount to elaborate systems of hermeneutics, aggressive and impious theories of interpretation. All observable phenomena are bracketed, in Freud's phrase, as manifest content. This manifest content must be probed and pushed aside to find the true meaning—the latent content beneath.[29]

The mastery of interpretation is a major note in Freud's work, but there are minor notes that disrupt this narrative of mastery and suggest a more complex view of interpretation.

Thinking of Freud in connection with Kafka's work has happened since even before the letter to his father was written in 1919. Kafka himself, after finishing "The Judgment" in 1912, jotted down in his journal, "Thoughts about Freud, of course."[30] The overwhelming stature of the father, his power over his son, his continued haunting of Kafka's psyche, their relationship structured as a battle—all recall Freud's account of the Oedipal complex. Stach suggests that "in the middle-class intellectual milieu of prewar Europe, it was impossible not to be aware of Freud's dethronement of the conscious mind."[31] In fact, as Sokel has pointed out, Kafka's letter is "a remarkable document, not least because of its cultural significance as one of the most consistent applications of Freud's theory of the Oedipus complex to one particular life,"[32] and this despite Kafka's many known criticisms of psychoanalysis and psychology.[33]

Studies connecting Freud and Kafka continue to appear even one hundred years after Kafka's own comments. Some works study the cultural and historical contexts in which Kafka and Freud lived as Jewish intellectuals in the turn-of-the-century Austrian-Czech milieu. Others connect psychoanalytic concepts with Kafka's stories. Still others connect their work thematically, most famously, perhaps, in Derrida's essay "Before the Law," in which he reads Kafka's work of that name together with Freud's myth of originary violence, of the killing of Moses.[34] Theodor Adorno warns that nothing "should tempt one to accept the thesis that Kafka has nothing to do with Freud,"[35] and Max Brod cautions against finding what he calls facile connections between Freud's ideas and Kafka's works:

> It seems impossible any longer to reject the connection with Freud's theories, particularly his explanation of the "subconscious." And yet I hesitate and must utter my protests against finding connections in this facile way, not least of all because Franz Kafka knew these theories very well and considered them always as a very rough and ready explanation which didn't do justice to detail, or rather to the real heartbeat of the conflict.[36]

However, here I would like to focus not on how Freud's theory of the subconscious might offer insight into Kafka's letter or his relationship with his father but rather on how the confrontation between Kafka and his father's modes of interpretation might help us to see and articulate a tension about interpretation in Freud's work, and how our attention to what Kafka performs in the writing of the letter—its undoing of the father's master narrative through the dialogization (to borrow Mikhail Bakhtin's term) of different voices and versions of father and son, its aim for approximation rather than mastery—might help us think about Freud's own performance of interpretation in *Interpretation of Dreams*. Kafka's works reveal the persistence and power of a hermeneutical drive that seeks mastery, even while they also suggest interpretation as a mode of engagement that enables us to maneuver the world's complexity, engage with others, and maintain our identities even in the face of hermeneutical tyranny. Like Freud, Kafka understands the presence of conflicting drives, but whereas Freud focuses on love and death, eros and thanatos, Kafka illuminates the ways in which the desire for complete interpretation drives our actions and hovers as an ever-present temptation. Reading Freud with an eye out for the hermeneutical drive, rather than Kafka with an eye out for the Oedipal complex, at the very least offers a less worn-out way to think about the relationship between the two and may offer some insight into the ways in which interpretive activity shapes our relationships, including the therapeutic relationship.

Psychoanalysis is, of course, founded on interpretation, the interpretation of dreams and symptoms. Philip Rieff comments that "the originality of psychoanalysis lies chiefly in its hermeneutic skill. This . . . is how we should read Freud's insistence that dream-interpretation is the keystone of the entire psychoanalytic structure."[37] It is a hermeneutic therapy based on the ability of the analyst to bring the patient to an acceptance of the analyst's interpretation of her situation. This interpretation uncovers her hidden desires, which find hallucinated fulfillment in her dreams or expression in her symptoms. The analyst serves as the reader of the patient's unconscious, an unconscious event that can never be directly accessed but can be known only indirectly through its representations. In fact, this indirectness is highlighted by the fact that it is not the dream itself that is the text to be interpreted but rather the patient's account of it.

Psychoanalysis reveals that unconscious desires play an important role in our actions, our dreams, and our linguistic constructions, but what sorts of desires are operative in the linguistic constructions that interpretations constitute? What sorts of unconscious desires are fulfilled in the activity of interpretation? What desires of the analyst are fulfilled, perhaps in a hallucinatory fashion, in his interpretation of dreams as hallucinatory wish fulfillments? What sorts of unconscious wishes are fulfilled, perhaps in a hallucinatory fashion, in the interpretation one makes of a literary text?

Freud's first analysis in *Interpretation of Dreams* provides an illuminating text for the exploration of these questions. In fact, Karl has made a connection specifically between this work and Kafka's "Letter to His Father," describing the latter as "a probing piece of self-analysis (similar to Freud's own self-analysis in the later 1890s leading to his *Interpretation of Dreams*)."[38] However, rather than focusing on their self-analyses, I want to look at a tension between Freud's descriptive and performative levels, between what he says about interpretation and what he performs. If Freud has taught us anything, he has taught us that what seems a tangential issue, an aside, is likely to be of utmost importance. I take this as grounds for focusing my attention on one of Freud's footnotes—the most seemingly insignificant of texts, relegated to the bottom of the page because it has been deemed not worthy of inclusion in the main text—in order to think about the desires that may be in play in interpretation.

Freud tells us that his main aim in *Interpretation of Dreams* is "to show that dreams are capable of being interpreted"[39] and further that "dreams really do have a meaning and that a scientific procedure for interpreting them is possible."[40] In presenting an interpretation of his own dream, Freud informs the reader that he has not offered a complete interpretation of the dream: "In scarcely any instance have I brought forward the *complete* interpretation of one of my own dreams, as it is known to me. I have probably been wise in not putting too much faith in my readers' discretion."[41] And yet Freud concludes the description and analysis of several details of his own dream with the statement, "I have now completed the interpretation of the dream."[42] He then adds, in a footnote, "though it will be understood that I have not reported everything that occurred to me during the process of interpretation."[43] Freud explains the wishes and intentions that are fulfilled in his dream but adds, "I will not pretend that I have completely uncovered the meaning of this dream, or that its interpretation is without a gap."[44] He could, he tells us, spend much more time analyzing it; however, "considerations which arise in the case of every dream of my own restrain me from pursuing my interpretive work."[45]

How do we as readers maneuver between the seemingly contradictory claims about completing and not completing the interpretation of his dream? From these comments, one might suppose that Freud has completely interpreted the dream but that he is keeping some of the information to himself for the sake of discretion. That is certainly one aspect of why he refrains from giving out certain information about his dream.

However, an earlier footnote suggests that there is more than a consideration for discretion that keeps Freud from giving a complete interpretation of his dream. Freud tells the reader,

> I had a feeling that the interpretation of this part of the dream was not carried far enough to make it possible to follow the whole of its concealed meaning. If I had pursued my comparison between the three women, it would have taken me far afield.—There is at least one spot in every dream at which it is unplumbable—a navel, as it were, that is its point of contact with the unknown.[46]

Mark Edmundson notes the intriguing nature of this footnote and its effect of eliciting desire in the reader to know more about this "unknown."[47] He asks, "How can Freud, the scientist in search of origins, speak so calmly of a region called 'the unknown'?"[48]

The question of the connection between science and the unknown is an intriguing one, but so is the question of how Freud can claim to have completely interpreted his dream—"I have now completed the interpretation of the dream"—if he has not accounted for everything in the dream and if every dream has an unfathomable point. In the concluding line of the chapter, he states that the important thing to understand is that "when the work of interpretation has been completed, we perceive that a dream is the fulfillment of a wish."[49] Is the transitive property at play here such that when the dream is perceived as a wish fulfillment, then the work of interpretation has been completed? It seems to be so, since a complete interpretation cannot mean accounting for everything in the dream or interpreting every part of it.

Might this not mean that the desire for a complete interpretation can be considered fulfilled, though really it is not, when the dream has been recognized as a wish fulfillment? In this situation, the interpretation of the dream itself functions as a dream in that it hallucinates the fulfillment of a desire—the desire for complete interpretation. Thus Freud's "complete interpretation" of his dream—his recognition of his dream as a wish fulfillment—constitutes a disguised and hallucinated fulfillment of his wish for complete interpretation. The desire for the completion of interpretation—a completion that is hallucinated rather than actually accomplished—is the desire that finds manifestation in the interpretive process.

Freud returns to his idea of the navel of a dream several hundred pages later in the text of *The Interpretation of Dreams*, but this time its reference appears in the main text—moved from the margins to the center. Here he revises his understanding of the navel in such a way that it, too, is brought from the murkiness of the margins to the clearer light of the center. He writes,

> There is often a passage in even the most thoroughly interpreted dream which has to be left obscure; this is because we become aware during the work of interpretation that at that point there is a tangle of dream-thoughts which cannot be unravelled and which moreover adds nothing to our knowledge of the content of the dream. This is the dream's navel, the spot where it reaches down into the unknown. . . . The dream-thoughts to which we are led by interpretation cannot, from the nature of things, have any definite endings; they are bound to branch out in every direction into the intricate network of our world of thought.[50]

Note that here the unfathomable part of the dream is translated into a mere tangle that would add nothing to the interpretation of the dream.

Thus there is a tension in Freud's work not only between the claim to have completely interpreted his dream and his juxtaposed statement that dreams can never be completely interpreted but also between the description of the navel as the point at which interpretation meets its limits and cannot interpret and the claim that the navel is the point where the dream is simply tangled and not worth unraveling anyway, since it would add nothing to the text.

Interestingly, Gayatri Chakravorty Spivak, in her preface to Derrida's *Of Grammatology*, focuses on this second reference to the dream's navel to explain Derrida's "procedure." Rather than recognizing in the navel the limits of the interpreter's capacities to interpret or analyze a text, she presents it as the place that locates the text's own point of imbalance and thus serves as the entryway to a deconstructive reading of it. She explains,

> Freud suggests further that . . . where the text looks supersmooth or superclumsy, is where the reader should fix his gaze, so that he does not merely read but deciphers the text, and sees its play within the open textuality of thought, language, and so forth within which it has only a provisionally closed outline. He catches this notion thus: "There is often a passage in even the most thoroughly interpreted dream which has to be left obscure. . . . At that point there is a tangle of dream-thoughts which cannot be unravelled and which moreover adds nothing to our knowledge of the content of the dream." . . . That passage is where we can provisionally locate the text's moment of transgressing the laws it apparently sets up for itself, and thus unravel—deconstruct—the very text. This illuminates the lines in Freud that follow the passage above: This is the dream's navel, the spot where it reaches down into the unknown. The dream-thoughts . . . cannot . . . have any definite endings: they are bound to branch out in every direction into the intricate networks of our world of thought.[51]

Note that the text is only "provisionally" closed: through deconstruction, it is made open. The navel is no longer the site of uninterpretability but of tangles that deconstruction itself can unravel. Spivak explains further the connection between Freud's navel and Derrida's procedure: "Freud has helped to push the procedure further—given him [Derrida] some means of locating the text's 'navel,' as it were, the moment that is undecidable in the text's apparent system of meaning, the moment that the text seems to transgress its own system values."[52] Here Freud's navel becomes not the point at which the interpreter must face the limits of interpretation itself—that which cannot be interpreted in the text—but instead the place where she finds its key, the key, that is, to deconstructing the logic of the text.

But Freud himself argues that there is not always such a key to dreams: "The question of whether it is possible to interpret every dream must be answered in the negative."[53] Again, the power of the interpreter, on the one hand, and the nature of the text and the limits of interpretation itself, on the other, are placed in tension: he tells us that whether we are able to interpret a dream "is thus a question of relative strength whether our intellectual interest, our capacity for self-discipline, our psychological knowledge, and our practice interpreting dreams enable us to master our internal resistance."[54] The question remains: is the reason we cannot interpret every dream because we are not strong enough to do so or because something in the dream itself is not amenable to a complete interpretation? And is it the case that not only can we not interpret every dream but also that no dream can be completely interpreted? These questions linger in Freud's text, never resolved once and for all. We are left with the following compromise of sorts: at least we can say, Freud tells us, that "it is always possible to go *some* distance: far enough, at all events, to convince ourselves that the dream is a structure with a meaning, and as a rule far enough to get a glimpse of what that meaning is."[55]

In this notion of a "glimpse" of meaning, we hear an echo of Kafka's approximation of the truth. Both Kafka and Freud acknowledge and declare the complexity of the "texts" under question—Kafka's relationship with his father, Freud's dreams—yet both still engage in interpretive efforts to understand them. Freud's complex and contradictory account of the relation of interpretive activity to the meaning of dreams—his claims to have completed interpretation of his own dream even while declaring that no dream can ever be completely interpreted—suggests that his internal battle is akin to the battle between Kafka and his father, between the hermeneutical mode of the tyrant who claims the power of complete interpretation and Kafka's own hermeneutical mode that recognizes the limits of its own capacity to interpret, the complexity of the text to be interpreted, and the limited possibilities—though possibilities nonetheless—for interpretive activity to offer at least a glimpse of meaning or an approximation of truth. Freud's footnote about the impossibility of completely interpreting his dream because of its unplumbable point undermines his own claims to have completely interpreted it and suggests a counterrecognition of the incomplete nature of the interpretation presented. Kafka's claim to be unable to give a complete interpretation of his relationship with his father, in his multivalent, polyglossic letter, undermines the father's claim that the matter is simple and amenable to singular interpretation.

Every interpretation runs the risk of functioning like a dream, of disguising its desire for complete interpretation and of hallucinating its fulfillment. Might it be that we are all driven by a desire for hermeneutical completion? And is it the failure to recognize this that leads us to misrecognize what can never be interpreted completely: the unknown, the unplumbable, in dreams, literary works, people? Freud's claim to have interpreted his dream completely reveals more about his hermeneutical desire than about the interpretation of dreams.

While Kafka offers us a family drama in which the drive for completion and the recognition of its impossibility are played by father and son, respectively, here Freud himself becomes the scene of the drama between these two modes of interpretation. He serves as an example of the temptation of claiming to have completed interpretation in conflict with the recognition that some things, like dreams, can never be fully interpreted. Read in this way, the relationship between analyst and patient becomes one of temptation for the analyst: he must resist the drive to claim to have completely interpreted the patient's dream or psychosis and must instead acknowledge the limited, perhaps even fragile nature of his interpretations and the limited comfort they might be able to offer. The claim to have completely interpreted the patient's dream is a hallucinated wish fulfillment on the part of the analyst.

Reading Freud through the lens of Kafka's landscape of interpretation, we see the struggle between the desire for complete interpretation and the acknowledgment that it is impossible. Adorno refers to Kafka's purported claim that "everything of his could be interpreted psychoanalytically except that this interpretation would in turn require further interpretation *ad indefinitum*"[56] and reveals thereby the resistance to closure and to claims to completion in Kafka's texts. Freud developed a science of interpretation; Kafka produced a literature of interpretation. Adorno describes them as "the explorer of the unconscious and the parabolist of impenetrability."[57] But in Kafka we find the insight to read Freud's fantasy of complete interpretation, even as countless critics have used Freud to read Kafka's nightmare of paternal power.

Let us return to where this chapter began—Kafka's comment that life is more than a puzzle—and add to it his comment that some approximation of the truth has been achieved by the correction made by the letter's rejoinder. Our excursion through Freud's *Interpretation of Dreams* highlighted the temptation that the fantasy of complete interpretation holds for us and the difficulty we have in sustaining the interpretive stance that keeps us engaged with the text, the other, or the world rather than bringing it to closure. In Kafka's qualifiers about what it is possible to achieve—that is, an approximation of the truth rather than a complete interpretation—we see a mode of resistance to hermeneutical tyranny. He acknowledges the possibility of multiple interpretations when he specifies that it is merely his opinion and not the only possible view, that something has been achieved by the letter. He highlights the partial nature of interpretations when he states that this something that has been achieved is not *the truth* but something that closely approximates it. He suggests the tentative and contingent nature of interpretations when he states that it is not a given that this approximation will improve things, only that it *might* do so. Finally, he acknowledges that mastery is not the goal but something smaller—just a little reassurance and the possibility of making things a little easier. Kafka's modest claims for the letter, his articulation of different views of the relationship, even within the space of the letter, suggest an effort to open up the space enclosed by the father's hermeneutical tyranny and a willingness to accept the impossibility of complete interpretation. At the same time, it is a means of self-defense against the hermeneutical tyranny of his father and, at times, a form of attack on his father—a subversive effort to keep open the hermeneutical arena that tyranny seeks to close down.

In presenting three versions of his father, himself, and their relationship, Kafka enacts his hermeneutics of complexity and plurality, in contrast to his father's hermeneutics of simplicity and singularity. The letter is both an effort at reconciliation and a move in the lifelong battle between father and son. When Kafka refers to the approximation of truth that his letter has achieved and the small comfort both he and his father might receive from it, there is a note of longing and loneliness. Even while the letter contributes to the battle between father and son, it also articulates the painful abyss between them. There is something about putting that into words that brings, at least to Kafka, some sense that he has drawn nearer to the truth, even if he can never get there, and in that there is some comfort. Kafka's claim that the letter has accomplished something is made before anyone has read it, which suggests that it is his writing of the letter rather than the expected or hoped-for reading of it that has accomplished something.

The letter outlines different modes of interpretation, ways of engaging with texts, the world, and others. What does this tell us about how we might read Kafka? Although the possible achievement to which Kafka refers comes from the writing of the letter, the ways in which he represents and interprets his relationship with his father suggest that he seeks to elicit some kinds of reading and interpretation while resisting others. The letter keeps open several possibilities of ways of reading it and in doing so resists a singular reading of it or of the relation between father and son. So, while the letter might resist our attempt to arrive at a definitive interpretation of it, it elicits our interpretive engagement as each new vision of the father-son relationship is brought into view. We can respond to our own hermeneutical drive to achieve a definitive interpretation by turning to tyranny, despair, or an ongoing engagement in the process of interpretation. Both tyranny and despair end the interpretive process. But Kafka's works choose the third option; his writing is an ongoing interpretive activity that keeps open his relation to the changing shape of truth.

In a letter to Milena, Kafka writes, "it's difficult to tell the truth, since there is only one truth, but that truth is alive and therefore has a lively, changing face."[58] This comment on the ontological shape of truth and on our relation to truth maps onto Kafka's suggestion to his father that the letter is a close enough approximation of the truth that it might achieve something. Kafka's sense of the truth—and of the world, others, and himself—forms his sense of what sort of interpretation is possible. Truth is not a puzzle to be solved but something changing and vital—it has a face. Likewise, he suggests that his works are also the sort of things that cannot be completely interpreted, and our reading should take the form of an ongoing interpretive engagement with them rather than an effort to arrive at a complete interpretation.

Chapter 2

The Power of Interpretation and the Interpretation of Power

Kafka's "The Judgment" and Bourdieu's Social Theory

Kafka considered his short story "The Judgment" to be his major breakthrough. He wrote it during the night of September 22–23, 1912, from ten o'clock in the evening until six o'clock the next morning.[1] In his diary, he noted that "only in this way can writing be done, only with such coherence, with such a complete opening out of the body and the soul."[2] Though Kafka was more satisfied with this story than with any of his other works, he found it bewildering. He wrote to Felice Bauer, the woman to whom he would twice be engaged and to whom the story is dedicated, "Can you discover any meaning in the 'Judgment'—some straightforward, coherent meaning that one could follow? I can't find any, nor can I explain anything in it."[3] Although he considered the process of writing the story to have had an admirable coherence, he could not find that same coherence of meaning in the story. Since "The Judgment" presented a hermeneutical challenge for its author, it is not surprising that readers have also been bewildered by it.

At the beginning of the story, the protagonist, Georg Bendemann, has just finished writing a letter to an old friend telling him of his recent engagement. He sits gazing out the window, looking at the river and the bridge below, thinking about his friend and the changing shape of their relationship over the years. At the end of the story, Georg flings himself over the side of this bridge to his death. The story is not very long, only seventeen typewritten pages by Kafka's count; a conversation between father and son is the only intervening event. And yet the distance between its beginning and end is immense. How does a character who seems to have everything going for him—a successful career, income from a flourishing business, an upcoming wedding—end up dead in a river? How does a lazy Sunday morning become deadly? Why does the conversation between father and son end fatally for Georg?

In "The Judgment" the power of interpretation becomes equivalent to the power over life and death. Kafka's "Letter to His Father" suggested the hermeneutical impotence he felt before the hermeneutical tyranny of his father; this impotence is magnified in the character of Georg. Like Kafka himself, Georg's interpretive and linguistic abilities dissolve in his conversation with his father. A confrontation that begins as the ostensibly innocent visit of a son to his father's room becomes a battle ending in the father's sentencing his son to death by drowning for being a devilish human being. What propels Georg's transformation from a successful businessman, engaged to a woman from a well-to-do family, to a son carrying out his father's death sentence?

To ask this question is to ask about the relation between interpretation and power. As in Kafka's "Letter to His Father," interpretive activity takes the form of a battle for power in "The Judgment." Interpretations serve as the tools of battle, and interpretive power is what each seeks to gain through the battle. This chapter explores how father and son seek to arm themselves and disarm each other by reinterpreting every relationship and circumstance to which their conversation turns, and how such reinterpretation is used as a means of obtaining, maintaining, and withholding power. Sociologist Pierre Bourdieu's work on struggles for power in the social realm and his disaggregation of different forms of capital—social, cultural, economic—help us to understand more deeply the process by which Georg's father strips him of his power, layer by layer and piece by piece. In short, this chapter aims to show, with the help of Bourdieu's discussion of power, the intricate and insidious ways in which interpretive activity is used in the battle for power between Georg and his father.

Bourdieu's Social Theory

Bourdieu's social theory helps us to unpack the overdetermined interaction between Georg and his father, the battle for power that occurs between them, and the changes in social status and capital that take place during their conversation, including the ways in which the father usurps all of Georg's relations and achievements, rendering them his own. In a 1986 lecture at the University of California, San Diego,[4] Bourdieu quoted *The Trial* in explaining the state's power to define reality:

> The state, which produces the official classification, is in one sense the supreme tribunal to which Kafka refers in *The Trial*, when Block says of the advocate who claims to be one of the "great Advocates": "any man can call himself 'great,' of course, if he pleases, but in this matter the Court tradition must decide."[5]

Bourdieu's reference to *The Trial* highlights the connection between power, authority, legitimation, and interpretation. Almost every person has the ability to claim that she is great, but the power to *impose* that interpretation as legitimate is quite a different matter. According to Bourdieu, the individual has no means to legitimate her claims when the recognized sources of legitimation are outside the self. Eric Santner highlights this connection between authority, legitimation, and interpretation: "One's performance must, in other words, be authorized. One cannot invest oneself with the authority to act as analyst or judge."[6] The matter of whether a person is great can be decided only by the court tradition in the world of *The Trial*, or by the state in the social world, as Bourdieu describes it, or, as it turns out, by the father in the world of "The Judgment." Only these figures have the power to impose interpretations as legitimate.

Like the individual who claims to be great but must await the declaration of the court, or the pronouncement of the state, to establish that she is, in fact, great, so too Georg can call himself successful, a good friend, a loyal son, but, as it turns out, he must await the declaration of his father to confirm or reject his self-interpretations. In the world of "The Judgment," it is Georg's father who has the power to determine reality, including Georg's status as a human being. Bourdieu's theory offers us a way to think about the complex and bewildering interaction between Georg and his father and to begin to understand just how it is that Georg's father gains such power over him.

Reading Kafka's story with Bourdieu's work also suggests the possibility of a dialogic relationship between theory and literature similar to the one that Bourdieu himself proposes between theory and empirical research.[7] In opposition to "theoretical theory," or theory that exists for itself and has little relation to the world, Bourdieu argues for theory that "emerges as a program of perception and of action . . . which is disclosed only in the empirical work which actualizes it."[8] That is, theory is not developed by a process of intellectual abstraction but rather through its engagement with detailed empirical work, in a process of proposal, actualization, and revision. Bourdieu prefers to see his theory as a set of "thinking tools" rather than "the kind of conceptual gobbledygook (*laïus*) that is good for textbooks."[9] When asked in an interview to explain the place of theory in his work, Bourdieu replied, "There is no doubt a theory in my work, or better, a set of *thinking tools* visible through the results they yield, but it is not built as such."[10] What might be taken as Bourdieu's theory serves as "a temporary construct which takes shape for and by empirical work,"[11] a construct that has "more to gain by confronting new objects than by engaging in theoretical polemics that do little more than fuel a perpetual, self-sustaining, and too often vacuous meta-discourse around concepts treated as intellectual totems."[12]

This sense of theory as temporary, subject to change as it encounters new objects, emergent rather than fixed, disclosed through a process rather than on display as an intellectual totem, connects with Kafka's sense of interpretation not as a fixed process but as a form of engagement that does not seek a determined end, though it does seek to draw near to the meaning of a text; that does not declare mastery but changes through new encounters; and that acknowledges a plurality of views rather than one authoritative voice even as it seeks to express its own view. In both models—Bourdieu's conception of theory and Kafka's vision of interpretation—the effort is not to control but to engage, not to seek power but understanding, not arrival but proximity, not a complete but just a better understanding. Interestingly, even though both eschew the desire for complete control, both are keenly interested in the process by which people and characters seek power over others and explore its dynamics in their work: Bourdieu through his social-scientific theoretical and empirical works and Kafka through his fiction and other writings.[13]

From Writing to Speaking, from Power to Powerlessness

"The Judgment" tells the story of Georg's journey from one area, or "field," to use Bourdieu's term, in which he has increasing capital, or resources, of all sorts to a field in which he is swiftly stripped of each type of capital, one by one. Bourdieu defines a "field" as "a social arena within which struggles or manoeuvres take place over specific resources or stakes or access to them."[14] The resources, or capital, in these struggles take various forms: economic, social, and symbolic. Georg's relationships with his friend, fiancée, and father can be seen as fields of power, as social arenas in which a struggle for power is taking place. In each case, Georg portrays himself as the one in control, the one with the upper hand, but he ends up losing his power. Finally, in his encounter with his father, he loses his life. His father's symbolic violence, his power to impose his interpretations as the only legitimate ones, fuels the process of Georg's divestment and propels him on his downward journey to his death.

Bourdieu defines "symbolic violence" as "the power which manages to impose meanings and to impose them as legitimate by concealing the power relations which are the basis of its source."[15] In his interactions with his friend, fiancée, and father, Georg attempts to impose some interpretation on the other person while concealing the symbolic violence inherent in his attempt. However, Georg hides the motivation for this imposition not only from others but also from himself. He misrecognizes—to use Bourdieu's term—his own attempts to maintain power by narrating them to himself in various legitimate guises: concern for his friend's self-respect, his fiancée's happiness, and his father's health. Ironically, the other characters see through Georg's rationalizations; by recognizing Georg's attempts at symbolic violence, they thereby thwart them, since for symbolic violence to work, the imposition of meaning must be viewed as legitimate by those on whom it is perpetrated. This presents a curious twist on Bourdieu's concept of "misrecognition": "the process whereby power relations are perceived not for what they objectively are but in a form which renders them legitimate in the eyes of the beholder."[16] In Kafka's story, it is the one attempting to use symbolic violence, Georg himself, who misrecognizes the attempt to impose interpretations as legitimate rather than those on whom the symbolic violence is supposed to work.

Censorship and Seduction

At the beginning of the story, we learn that, in the past three years, Georg's "position in life [has] changed a lot."[17] He has become the head of the family business and of the household, displacing his father in both roles. Profits from the business have increased, and the staff has been doubled. Georg is about to marry a woman from a well-to-do family and thereby increase his social capital. The opening line tells the reader that it is the "very height of spring" (77), highlighting the atmosphere of new growth and the promise of more to come. As Georg thinks to himself, "no doubt about it, further progress [lies] just ahead" (79).

Georg has just finished writing a letter to an old friend, who, in contrast, has experienced a worsening of his situation in life. He runs a business that has "long been going downhill" (77). He is "wearing himself out to no purpose" (77)—there is no sense that his situation might improve. His declining health is evident by the fact that "his skin [is] growing so yellow as to indicate some latent disease" (77). His isolation is thorough, since he has "no regular contact with the colony of his fellow countrymen out there" (77), has "almost no social intercourse with Russian families" (77), and is resigning himself to life as a bachelor. The friend is bankrupt physically, economically, and socially: he has poor health, little money, few meaningful relationships, and no social status.

However, all the information the reader receives about the friend comes through Georg. There is something conspicuously odd about how Georg enumerates to himself the ways in which his friend is failing as he reflects on his own successes. Bourdieu argues that individuals "constantly work to differentiate themselves from their closest rivals in order to reduce competition and to establish a monopoly."[18] Georg's description of his friend can be seen as Georg's attempt to push down a rival rather than to empathize with a friend. Georg thinks of his friend in terms of decline in an effort to bolster his view of himself as someone on the path of increasing economic and social capital. In so doing, he reveals the instability of that increase and also the instability of his very self. Thomas Luckmann and Peter Berger note that "if status is relatively uncertain and relatively inconsistent, conditions are created that are unfavorable for the consistency and stability of the self."[19] We shall see that Georg's need to narrate his friend in terms of decline is a futile attempt to preserve a failing sense of himself as a success. His preoccupation with his friend's decline suggests a preoccupation with the instability of his own position and the possibility of his own decline.

Georg censors the information he provides his friend, particularly that relating to Georg himself. He formulates numerous arguments for himself as to why he cannot advise his friend to come home, despite his friend's apparent decline in Russia. Most of Georg's arguments rest on the premise that such advice would make his friend feel like a failure and that returning home would not necessarily improve his friend's situation. Georg tells himself that "for such reasons, supposing one wanted to keep up correspondence with him, one could not send him any real news such as could be frankly told to the most distant acquaintance" (78). The assumption that his friend's decline means that he cannot be told any real news is striking. Might not news of home be welcome to him, reminding him of the connections he still has there? His friend has "no inkling" (79) of the improvement in Georg's position in life because Georg has refrained from telling him about it. Georg wants to preserve the "idea of the home town which his friend must have built up to his own content during his long interval" (79). Note that Georg imputes to his friend a kind of fantasy creation in terms of the idea of home—a fantasy that Georg must take pains not to shatter. Georg confines "himself to giving his friend unimportant items of gossip such as rise in the memory when one is idly thinking things over on a quiet Sunday" (79). Of course, "unimportant items," particularly those that arise when one is thinking idly, are just the sort of items to which attention should be paid. And this, in fact, is what the friend does when he begins to take an interest in an engagement that Georg has mentioned.

The piece of news that Georg most strenuously resists telling his friend is his engagement to Frieda Brandenfeld. Georg thinks that his friend's illusory picture of home would be shattered by news of Georg's engagement and describes his censorship as an attempt to spare his friend that heartbreak. However, as it turns out, it is *Georg's* idea of home that is an illusion, just as his idea of himself as the protector of his friend's illusions turns out to be illusory. Georg projects onto his friend his own process of building up illusions to protect himself from the truth. By the end of the story, it is Georg's illusions that are shattered by his father's pronouncements rather than the friend's illusions being shattered by Georg's announcements.

The censorship that Georg has exercised in previous letters begins to backfire when the friend takes an interest in the seemingly unimportant engagement Georg does mention. Censorship is the means by which Georg has attempted to preserve or control his friend's view of Georg's world. Georg misrecognizes the symbolic violence he is perpetrating on his friend by depicting it to himself as concern for his friend's psychological and emotional welfare. Georg's censorship serves to maintain the social capital that his relationship with his friend represents by limiting the amount of legitimate knowledge to which the friend has access.

However, more seems to be at stake than simply the preservation of a friendship that from all appearances does not provide Georg with much by way of companionship or intimacy. What may also be at stake is hinted at by Kafka's description of the story: "The story may be a journey around father and son, and the friend's changing shape may be a change in perspective in the relationship between father and son."[20] The friendship's importance can be seen in its connection to the relationship between Georg and his father: it is the capital over which they will struggle—with life-or-death consequences.

Georg's censorship also threatens his relationship with his fiancée, Frieda. She states that she has a right to know all of Georg's friends. However, giving Frieda access to his friend would threaten Georg's imagined position as his friend's sole informer and would shatter the image of himself he has tried to present in his letters to his friend. His relationship with his friend is maintained through the control of information that is given to him; Frieda's entrance into the relationship would threaten Georg's role as censor.

Frieda recognizes the incompatibility of Georg's engagement and his friendship when she states, "Since your friends are like that, Georg, you shouldn't ever have got engaged at all" (80). Georg attempts to suppress Frieda's resistance to his written censorship with physical censorship by placing his mouth against hers and thereby preventing her from speaking.[21] According to Sokel, this act both censors her and reveals his animosity toward her: "The very manifestation of his love acts as both a cover-up and an unacknowledged expression of his true hostility toward the fellow conspirator in his 'guilt.'"[22] However, his efforts prove to be unsuccessful; Frieda is able to voice her protest despite Georg's physical censorship and despite her state of sexual arousal: "when, breathing quickly under his kisses, she manage[s] to say, 'I really do feel offended.'"[23] Georg has failed to silence her dissent through either physical force or sexual seduction, and he capitulates to her request to tell his friend of their engagement. In attempting to use seduction as a means of enforcing censorship, Georg instead submits to Frieda's power, which puts an end to his censorship, both in the realm of their relationship and in all of Georg's relationships. Georg's failure to censor Frieda leads to his ceasing to censor the information he sends to his friend. Georg's inability to impose his will by means of sexual power, combined with his susceptibility to Frieda's sexual power, contributes to Georg's final hermeneutical impotence at the end of the story. Kafka connects Georg's fiancée to his subsequent death when he writes in his diary on August 14, 1913, "Georg goes to pieces because of his fiancée."[24]

Georg agrees to give up censoring the information he sends his friend and says to himself: "That's the kind of man I am and he'll just have to take me as I am. . . . I can't cut myself to another pattern that might make a more suitable friend for him" (80). However, this is precisely what he has been doing. He has censored his letters, he tells himself, in order to make himself a more suitable friend. He has been cutting to a precise pattern all the information he has sent to his friend, particularly that about himself. He has been engaged in symbolic violence against his friend as a means of preserving his own sense of himself as a successful man. Georg agrees to give up his means of power in his relationship to his friend in order to maintain the social, economic, and symbolic capital that comes from his engagement to Frieda.

In writing to his friend, Georg narrates his engagement in terms of an increase in social capital for his friend: "Instead of a quite ordinary kind of friend you will now have in me a happy friend. Besides that, you will acquire in my fiancée . . . a genuine friend of the opposite sex, which is not without importance to a bachelor" (80). Though Georg's decision to tell the friend about his engagement seems to accompany a decision to let go of his friend's approval, he narrates it in such a way as to preserve the idea that his main concern is for his friend's welfare. He decides that "it really could not involve him in much trouble were he to send the news to his friend" (80), though, as his labyrinthine rationalizations for not telling his friend suggest and as the end of the story reveals, this is precisely what begins the process that ends in his death. Georg writes to his friend of his engagement because of Frieda's protests, and it is purportedly to tell his father of the letter that he enters his father's room, where he is sentenced to death.

The Battle for Power

Upon entering his father's room, Georg's interpretations come under fire and the hierarchy of power is reversed. At the beginning of the story, the friend, the father, and Georg had each experienced a change in social status: The friend had "gone downhill" from success to failure in his business. He had left friends and ended up in isolation. He had traveled away from the comforts of home to the remoteness of Russia, from the realm of marriage to the territory of bachelorhood, from the climate of health to the domain of disease. He had traded his well-known childhood face for a foreign-looking beard and jaundiced skin. Georg's father had descended from his position as master of his house, head of his business, and healthy husband to being a dependent, old widower living in a darkened room and needing his son's aid. In contrast, Georg had ascended to a position of power and success in the family business, moved from dependent son to head of the household, from bachelorhood to engagement.

Or at least this is how Georg wants to view things. In his room, in the safety of isolation where people can wave to him from the street below but not speak to him, where his communication with others takes the form of writing rather than speech, where there is no one to challenge his interpretations or replace them—here Georg is in control. However, once he leaves this world and enters the world of the father, in which the mode of communication is dialogue rather than monologue, Georg loses both his bearings and his stature. As Sokel notes, "Entering his father's back room, Georg confronts a world, new and strange."[25] Georg's encounter with his father brings about a reversal of the ascents and descents of

Georg, his friend, and his father. Georg's movement from his own room to his father's moves him from the "very height of spring" to the depths of decay and powerlessness, from the expansive view of the river and bridge to the darkened back room of his father, from the realm where he is in control to one in which he loses all power.

The reason Georg enters his father's room is unclear; the text tells us it was unusual for Georg to go to his father's room since "there was in fact no need for him to enter it" (80). Georg says to his father, "I really only wanted to tell you . . . that I am now sending the news of my engagement to St. Petersburg . . . before I posted the letter I wanted to let you know" (81). Why would he want to let his father know that he is finally telling his friend about his engagement and why before sending the letter? Implied is a sense that the father is somehow connected to either his relationship with his friend or his relationship with his fiancée, that his father knows that Georg has been keeping the news from his friend, and that Georg wants his father's approval for finally revealing this information to the friend. Like Kafka with his own father, and Joseph K. with the court in *The Trial*, Georg wants the approval of a higher authority, his father, and, more specifically, he wants to be declared innocent. Just as Joseph K.'s relentless pursuit of the court's acquittal suggests insecurity about his innocence, so Georg's wanting to let his father know about the letter reveals an unease about it.

When Georg tells his father the reason why he decided to inform his friend of his engagement, he leaves out any mention of his fiancée's request that he do so. He says, "I've been thinking it over. If he's a good friend of mine, I said to myself, my being happily engaged should make him happy too. And so I wouldn't put off telling him any longer" (82). Hiding the fact that it was the fiancée who persuaded Georg to tell his friend of the engagement, Georg characterizes his decision instead as the result of his having thought it over. His editing out of the fiancée's role in his decision shows Georg's censorship at work and suggests that there is some guilt involved in his having acquiesced to her supplications. Both narrations—to his friend of his engagement and to his father of his decision to tell his friend—omit the instigating force of the fiancée's request. Once again, in playing the censor, even as he plays the role of one who has given up censorship, Georg reveals the instability of his situation and indicates that something would be at risk if the truth were known.

When Georg first enters the room, his father seems more like a pathetic old man than an authority figure. Like the friend, the father has experienced a radical decline on multiple fronts. He is no longer head of the household or the family business; he has lost his wife and moved to the status of widower. His health is failing, and he has a "defect of vision" (81). The remains of his breakfast reveal his weak appetite. He is not yet dressed, and, as Georg discovers, his underwear is "not particularly clean" (84). He tells Georg at one point, "I'm not equal to things any longer, my memory's failing. I haven't an eye for so many things any longer" (82). He sits surrounded by "mementoes of Georg's dead mother" (81), indicating his withdrawal from active involvement in the everyday world. The room, overshadowed by a high wall outside, is dark despite the sunny morning. The narrative details at this point in the story suggest that this is an aging parent who has slipped into the dark world of his own memories.

However, inserted into this depiction of the father are details that hint at quite a different interpretation of the father. Georg finds the room "*unbearably* dark" and thinks to himself, "My father is still a giant of a man . . . how solidly he sits there with his arms crossed" (81). Georg is "trying to meet his father's eye" (81), which implies that he is not easily able to do so. These details trouble the surface of the narrative and the reader's interpretation of the father, and they reveal Georg's ambivalent feelings toward him.

Of particular significance in this context is the changing depiction of the father's newspaper.[26] When Georg walks in, his father is trying to read the newspaper in the dark room, but in order to do so he has to hold it "to one side before his eye in an attempt to overcome a defect of vision" (81). The darkness and poor eyesight suggest the father's failing health. However, the newspaper suddenly becomes "enormous" (82) as the father begins interrogating Georg. Further, at this point the father puts his spectacles away as if he no longer needs them. Later, the father throws off the bedcovers and tosses a sheet of the newspaper toward Georg. Three aspects of the newspaper are interesting to note here: First, Georg did not notice that his father had "taken to bed with him" (87) this sheet of newspaper, even though Georg had put him in the bed and even though it was "enormous." Second, the newspaper is old and unknown to Georg, suggesting some hidden source of knowledge to which only his father has access. Finally, the father tosses the newspaper aside, declaring that, in fact, he has not been reading newspapers but rather, as Georg cries out, has been "lying in wait" (87) for his son, so the newspaper reading has been a ruse in the battle for power. Georg initially reads or interprets the newspaper so that it fits in with his narrative of the failing father, but this reading fails as his father rewrites even the symbolic meaning of the newspaper itself.

Georg's response to and interpretation of the newspaper parallels his response to and interpretation of his father. When his father seems to be a decrepit old man, the newspaper is connected with his father's lack of vision. When his father seems to be a "giant of a man," the newspaper becomes enormous. When he misinterprets his father's willingness to go to bed, he has not noticed that his father has taken the newspaper with him. When he can no longer read his father's actions, the name of the newspaper is entirely unknown to Georg. Finally, when the newspaper is tossed away by the father, it is then that Georg himself is also tossed away by the father.

Georg's shifting view of his father, mirrored in his shifting view of the newspaper, also mirrors the hermeneutical uncertainty of Kafka's readers: Is the father senile? Or does he know something we do not know? The father's startling question, "Do you really have this friend in St. Petersburg?" (82), brings uncertainty about the father's senility and the trustworthiness of Georg's perspective to the forefront of readers' minds. Suddenly we are made aware of a possibility not even imagined until this point in the narrative: perhaps Georg has just made up this friend! Everything in the story up to now has revolved around the friend, underscoring both his importance and his existence. The father's question was not even in the "universe of possible questions," to borrow Bourdieu's phrase from an essay on Flaubert.[27]

To add to the reader's uncertainty is the fact that the question, as Sokel points out, can be interpreted in two different ways. The question represents an example of the story's "two-layered duality of perspectives linguistically expressed by the coincidence of literal and figurative, or basic and derived, meanings."[28] The question's two meanings indicate a difference of emphasis, one concerned with fact, which is related to Georg, and the other concerned with meaning and truth, which is related to the father. In this first meaning, the question could be rephrased as, "Is there a person in St. Petersburg whom you call your friend?" Or, "Does this person really exist?" When read this way, the question could point to a loss in the father's memory and the onset of senility. It could also suggest that Georg has completely made up this figure. The second meaning of the question relates to the nature of Georg's relationship with the friend: "Is this person whom you call your friend truly your friend?" Here Sokel sees a search for the truth of the relationship between Georg and his friend. The father's insistence that Georg tell him the truth could point to either meaning of the question; however, Georg interprets it as one of fact: whether there is such a person living in Russia.

Georg's immediate response to the question is odd. Rather than answering the question, Georg becomes embarrassed and immediately reassures his father of his value: "Never mind my friends. A thousand friends wouldn't make up to me for my father" (82). He tries to read the question as indicative not of the father's doubt about Georg's veracity or sense of judgment about the friend but rather of his insecurity about being an important person in Georg's life. Suddenly Georg becomes the overly solicitous son, concerned about his father's health and deciding on the spot that his father will come and live with him when he gets married. This role-playing functions like Bourdieu's "strategies of condescension," in which

> agents who occupy a higher position in one of the hierarchies of objective space symbolically deny the social distance between themselves and others, a distance which does not thereby cease to exist, thus reaping the profits of the recognition granted to a purely symbolic denigration of distance ("she is unaffected," "he is not highbrow" or "stand-offish," etc.) which implies a recognition of distance.[29]

By taking on the role of caring, solicitous son, Georg puts his father in the role of helpless, elderly father and thereby tries to reinforce his own position as head of the household. Though he seems to bridge the power gap between them, Georg is actually reinforcing his power by putting his father in the subservient role of an old, senile widower. In putting his father to bed, Georg takes on the caregiving role and tries to render his father a child who needs him.

However, his father does not accept this role reversal, this complete loss of power. He asks Georg, "Am I well covered up?" This question, like the father's previous one, can be read in two ways: "Are the blankets on the bed covering me up well?" or "Have you ousted me from my position and sent me into obscurity or death?" The first is a literal interpretation of the question; the second is a figurative one. The question exposes Georg's attempt to put his father in a subservient position: "You wanted to cover me up, I know, my young sprig, but I'm far from being covered up yet. And even if this is the last strength I have, it's enough for you, too much for you" (84). Georg's strategy of condescension backfires and is revealed as a grasping for power. All of a sudden, the father, who had seemed near death—"it almost looked, on closer inspection, as if the care he meant to lavish there on his father might come too late" (84)—becomes an all-powerful figure.[30] And the friend, whom the father has until now seemed not to remember, is suddenly described by the father as "a son after [his] own heart" (85). Georg the successful businessman is transformed by his father's words into a "young sprig," and the friend in Russia with failing health, no social interaction, and a miserably failing business is suddenly transformed into the father's true son.

Georg's attempt at symbolic violence—to impose on his friend a certain interpretation of the world, home, and his engagement, and to impose on his father a certain interpretation of their roles as father and son—is recognized by his father as illegitimate, rather than misrecognized as legitimate. The father says,

> "You've been playing him false all these years . . . that's why you had to lock yourself up in your office . . . just so that you could write your lying little letters to Russia. But thank goodness a father doesn't need to be taught to see through his son." (85)

Despite his previous claim of failing eyesight, the father now sees all too clearly. His power of sight seems to come from the mere fact of being Georg's father, from his very person, much as Kafka's father's power seems to come from his person rather than from any legitimate claim to authority. Not only can he see Georg, he can see through him. Each of Georg's sources of power is now reinterpreted by his father as a facade in such a way that Georg loses power and accrues guilt.

Georg's rising social status as an engaged man becomes reinterpreted by his father as his having succumbed to temptation, an instance of weakness rather than power. The father declares that Georg's relationship with Frieda results from his having given in to her powers of seduction and is merely his attempt to "make free with her undisturbed" (85). The father declares,

> "Because she lifted up her skirts . . . because she lifted up her skirts like this, the nasty creature," and mimicking her he lifted his shirt so high that one could see the scar on his thigh from his war wound, "because she lifted her skirts like this and this you made up to her, and in order to make free with her undisturbed you have disgraced your mother's memory, betrayed your friend, and stuck your father into bed so he can't move. But he can move, or can't he?" (85)[31]

His engagement is evidence of not only his weakness in the face of seduction but also his triple betrayal: of his mother, his friend, and his father. Three times the father mentions Frieda's lifting her skirts and mimics this lifting with an accompanying "like this." With each repetition the picture is further embellished with an additional phrase—"because she lifted up her skirts," "because she lifted up her skirts like this, nasty creature," "because she lifted up her skirts like this and this you made up to her"—as if, in the process of imagining the scene, the father himself is getting more and more caught up in the image of it, and with increasing condemnation of his son.

Interestingly, the father's "skirts" are also lifted up at three moments in the story. When he rises to meet Georg, after the latter has just entered the room, the father's "heavy dressing gown swung open as he walked and the skirts of it fluttered around him" (81). Even a non-Freudian could hardly resist interpreting Georg's response to this—that his father is "still a giant of a man"—as having to do with his father's genitals. Georg's attention is again drawn to what is under the skirts of his father's dressing gown after Georg takes it off his father. He notices that his father's linen underpants are "not particularly clean" (84), a fact for which he immediately takes responsibility, deciding that "it should have certainly been his duty to see that his father had clean changes of underwear" (84), rendering his father like an infant who needs his diaper changed. Finally, his father mimics Frieda's lifting her skirts as a rhetorical move to underscore the fact that Georg has disgracefully succumbed to her sexual power.

The father elicits two visions of Frieda when he tells Georg, "Just take your bride on your arm and try getting in my way! I'll sweep her from your very side, you don't know how!" (86). If Georg tries to replace the image of Frieda provocatively lifting her skirts with the more respectable image of Georg walking with her as his bride, he will find himself suddenly without any woman at all. Whereas Georg sought to preserve illusions, his father seeks to expose what he considers Georg's most disreputable illusion: that he is marrying out of love rather than lust. In the father's view, it is the engagement, rather than the friendship, that should have been forgone. (Of note, Frieda herself also sees the incompatibility of Georg's friendship and his engagement when she suggests that he should not have become engaged if he had friends like that.) It is Georg's succumbing to Frieda's sexual power that his father identifies as the source of Georg's other evils and for which the father, in the end, condemns him.[32]

With his father's rise to power, Georg suddenly remembers that "a long time ago he had firmly made up his mind to watch closely [his father's] every least movement so that he should not be surprised by any indirect attack, a pounce from behind or above" (85). The relationship between father and son is a full-fledged battle for power in which vigilance is key. All sources of power and all forms of capital are up for reinterpretation. The father appropriates Georg's sources of social and economic capital one by one, as if disarming him of his weapons. The profits the business made under Georg's direction are redescribed as merely the result of Georg's "finishing off deals that [his father] had prepared for him" (86). His engagement is a succumbing to temptation, and his friendship is a lie.

Georg's entrance into his father's room has brought more than a reversal of fortune: it is a descent into a realm in which Georg loses all hermeneutical power and becomes the impotent subject.

Georg's sources of power are shown to be not only facades but also sources of his father's power. His father asserts that he has the power to "sweep [Frieda] from [Georg's] very side," even after she has become Georg's bride. Georg's inability to keep his fiancée, even once she has become his bride, underscores his impotence. In contrast to his son's impotence in relation to his fiancée, the father claims to have been given his strength by his wife. The father enumerates Georg's relationships and reinterprets them as sources of his own power: "Your mother has given me so much of her strength that I've established a fine connection with your friend and I have your customers here in my pocket!" (86). The repetition of "your" resounds with irony, for Georg's mother has given his father the strength to oppose Georg, his friend is now his father's ally, and his customers are in his father's pocket.

This image of the father having Georg's customers in his pocket is surprising until one realizes that pockets are often strongly connected with power in Kafka's works.[33] The father's declaration that he has Georg's customers in his pocket is a sign of his power over Georg. Earlier in the story, Georg revealed the letter he had just written to his friend by lifting it slightly from his pocket and letting it slip back down. This literal exposure of what was in his pocket serves as a figurative exposure of his source of power, making him vulnerable to his father's attack. For it is only in writing, rather than in conversation with his father, that Georg, like Kafka himself, seems able to exercise power; in the realm of conversation, with his fiancée and with his father, he collapses.

Further, his undressing of his father can be seen as an attempt to literally "de-pocket" or disempower him, a connection that is reinforced when Georg says to himself, "'He has pockets even in his shirt!' . . . and believe[s] that with this remark he could make him an impossible figure for all the world" (86). The man who has pockets not only in his trousers but "even in his shirt" has multiple sources of power. A man's pockets are usually close to his genitals, which are, as we have seen, another source of the father's power in this story. Pockets are also places where people can hide things; in this case, the father has hidden his power in all his pockets. He has sources of power, or pockets, of which Georg had no inkling.

The father's connection with the friend is also significant. Georg's attempts to control the friend's view of the world turn out to be impotent efforts. His friend now seems to be his father's ally; in fact, his father claims to be the friend's representative. With this all-powerful representative, the friend ascends from his position as a man "who had obviously run off the rails" (77) to one who, according to the father, "knows everything a thousand times better" (87) than Georg does himself. Georg has conceived of the friend only moments earlier as "lost in the vastness of Russia . . . at the door of an empty, plundered warehouse . . . among the wreckage of his showcases, the slashed remnants of his wares, the falling gas brackets" (85), barely able to stand. And yet this picture more aptly describes Georg's own situation of forsakenness.[34]

Georg portrays others in terms that reinforce his own power—for example, his father as an invalid, his friend as lost and alone, his fiancée as pliable with kisses. However, his father's hermeneutical abilities prove stronger than Georg's. Even Georg's attempt to make fun of his father, by joking that the friend knows everything not a thousand times better but "ten thousand times" better, backfires on him, as "in his very mouth the words turned into deadly earnest" (87). The image of the friend crumpling Georg's unopened letters in his left hand while holding up the father's in his right provides a stark contrast to Georg's earlier image of him as so influenced by Georg's letters that Georg has to censor their content to protect his friend's fragile state. Georg the censor has actually been the one censored by his friend. Georg has become the writer of impotent letters, while his father has become the writer of triumphant letters that win the battle even before being read.

In short, according to his father, Georg's friend is his father's ally, Georg's economic capital is in his father's pocket, and his bride-to-be is easily swept from Georg's side by his father. Though Georg tries to resist these imperialistic interpretations, making a grimace of disbelief—at one point, he even tries calling his father's whole act a comedy—his father merely nods, "confirming the truth [and power] of his words" (86). His father has redefined all of Georg's capital such that it becomes his own and, in so doing, reveals that he is the one with symbolic capital—that is, the power to interpret everything and to impose those interpretations as legitimate. Even Georg's informing his father about the letter becomes reclassified by the father as a request for his advice. Georg had described his visit to his father as motivated merely by the desire to tell him that he was sending his friend news of his engagement: "I really only wanted to tell you . . . that I am now sending the news of my engagement to St. Petersburg" (81). However, his father reinterprets that action as a request: "How you amused me today, coming to ask me if you should tell your friend about your engagement" (87). The father's power to reinterpret everything about Georg extends even to his motivation for telling his father about writing the letter. That his father can reinterpret even what motivated his son's entrance into his room reveals the extent of his power. Not only that, his father has known this request was coming: "For years I've been waiting for you to come with some such question!" (87). The fact that he has been waiting for years suggests the energy that has been brewing during the waiting and that erupts in the conversation.

As the "Letter to His Father" revealed and as this reading of "The Judgment" shows, for Kafka "power" and "father" are almost synonymous. Sokel extends this correlation through the course of Kafka's work: "From 'The Judgment' to Kafka's last work, 'Josephine,' this father figure possesses a power that, however unseen, mysterious, and generalized it becomes, retains a fundamental effectiveness that plays havoc with the assumptions, opinions, and claims of Kafka's protagonist."[35] Power is infused into the words the father speaks. For "the power of words to *do* things is a function of the authority and appropriateness of the speaker, not to mention the appropriateness of audience and context . . . the essential point is that words *do* have power."[36] It is no wonder that the father's verdict and sentencing of Georg prove all-powerful. The father's statements are not merely words with a certain linguistic meaning; Bourdieu reminds us that "utterances are not only (save in exceptional circumstances) signs to be understood and deciphered, they are also . . . *signs of authority*, intended to be believed and obeyed."[37] The father's reinterpretations of all Georg's sources of power have redescribed them as the father's sources of power and thereby wrested them from Georg, leaving him destitute. And the father has done so in a way that Georg finds irresistibly believable and requiring his obedience.

Power, according to Bourdieu, should be viewed not as a substance but as a factor of relatedness: "To say for example of someone that he has power . . . is to think of power as a substance, a thing which certain people hold, preserve, transmit,"[38] and this, according to Bourdieu, is a mistaken view. An individual is powerful because of her position in society, her relation to the people and institutions around her, and the esteem with which she is viewed. Despite Georg's apparently high level of social and economic capital, the father's high level of symbolic capital—that is, his high stature and authority, his ability to claim his interpretations as the legitimate ones—proves stronger.

Thus, the father ascends from his powerless state as a widower, aging dependent parent, and ousted head of the business and household to the position of a judge whose words have immediate power to compel action. The father is transformed in the encounter into a powerful godlike figure, while Georg's agency is subsumed by the encounter. As Charles Bernheimer suggests, "His father's command has taken the place of [Georg's] autonomous will. . . . His perspective has taken over Georg and become one with the core of his being."[39] Georg's ascent and his father's descent prior to the beginning of the story are reversed as a result of this encounter: the father rises to the height of a divine-like judge and Georg is driven down to his death.[40] Georg, the successful young businessman with the power to attract a woman from a well-to-do family, to increase his family business's turnover fivefold, for whom "further progress lay just ahead" (79), becomes powerless to do anything but carry out his father's declaration: "I sentence you now to death by drowning!" (87).

Therefore, when Georg's father says to him, "An innocent child, yes, that you were, truly, but still more truly have you been a devilish human being!" (87), he is not merely stating an opinion; he is outlining the trajectory of Georg's descent from innocent child to devilish human being and defining Georg's very self. According to Peter Berger, "the family is . . . the principal agency for the definition and maintenance of private identity,"[41] but Georg's father becomes the principal agency for the definition and then *dissolution* of Georg's identity as Georg finds himself urged from the room as if his agency itself has been overtaken. Georg's role of dutiful son is redefined as the mask of a devilish human being, and the result is disastrous for him. Bourdieu highlights the power and destructive capacity of naming: "The power of naming, in particular of naming the unnamable, that which is still unnoticed or repressed, is a considerable power. Words, said Sartre, can wreak havoc."[42] In Georg's case, they certainly do. The father's discourse is the authoritative discourse. His words have the power of God in Genesis; the boundary between language and the physical world disappears and words function like hands, making and unmaking with their utterance. However, in this case they do not call Adam and Eve into being but drive Georg to his death. The story can be seen as an antibildungsroman: the self is not educated and formed by the other but rather uneducated, unformed, deconstructed by the other.

In using the language of the court—"I sentence you now to death by drowning"—Georg's father takes on absolute authority. The language of the father, like the language of the state, is "an almost divine discourse which assigns to everyone an identity."[43] Like Kafka, who told his father, "For me as a child everything you called out to me was positively a heavenly commandment, I never forgot it, it remained for me the most important means of forming a judgment of the world,"[44] so Georg responds to his father's judgment as if it were a heavenly commandment to kill himself. He is assigned the identity of "devilish human being" and, as if by divine intervention, finds himself driven from the room, down the stairs, and out into the street. Georg is overpowered by his father's sentence, and this completes his hermeneutical failure. Unable to reinterpret his father's words, he submits to his father's interpretation of him. He has no way to resist the crushing power of his father's words.

Or does he? Might there be some means of resistance left for him? Might the father not be the all-powerful judge, after all? As Georg flees the room, his father falls down on the bed, the noise of which rings in Georg's ears. This bed was a symbol of the father's decline earlier in the story when Georg put him to bed after noticing his frail health. The father makes a connection between his bed and a grave with his question about being well covered up, connoting not only his being tucked into bed but also his burial. The father suggests that this battle may be his last with his earlier declaration, "Even if this is the last strength I have, it's enough for you, too much for you." These narrative details indicate that the father has used his last bit of strength to condemn his son and has no more energy left.

Whether it is because he is no longer in his father's physical presence or because his father's collapse lessens the power his words have over Georg, by the time Georg reaches the bridge, his agency returns to him. Georg is dissolved in the encounter with his father; his feeling of being "urged from the room" (87) and "driven toward the water" (88) reveals his *lack* of agency. However, some element of his agency has been restored as he swings himself over the side of the bridge. When he hangs from the bridge, the story tells us that he waits until the noise of the traffic will cover the sound his dropping into the water will make: "With weakening grip he was still holding on when he spied between the railings a motor-bus coming which would easily cover the noise of his fall" (88). Though his grip is weakening, he has enough strength to time his letting go. This is not someone who is being driven by forces he cannot resist; rather, Georg is choosing the timing of his death. Judith Butler underscores the importance of this shift in agency: "Although the strong wind of the father's condemnation forces Georg out of the room and down the stairs, the suicidal acrobatics that he performs are his own voluntary action, one performed for his father."[45] Kafka highlights this agency in a letter to Felice when he points out that the verb he uses here is "to drop," not "to fall": "The final word in the penultimate sentence should read 'drop' [*hinabfallen*] not 'fall' [*hinfallen*]."[46]

That Georg's agency has returned enough for him to choose the timing of his drop into the water is very important and something to which many critics do not attend. It sheds light on Georg's last words: "Dear parents, I have always loved you, all the same" (88).[47] These are not the words of a son overpowered into submission, nor are they the words of an individual whose consciousness has been dissolved and overtaken by the words of another. Rather, these words of love resist his father's judgment of him as a devilish human being. Thus, Georg's final act proves his father's judgment of him wrong. For by carrying out his father's *sentence*—death by drowning—Georg proves his father's *judgment*—devilish human being—wrong. Georg's "self-execution appears as a last act of protest and as a disproof of the justice of the judgment."[48] He who has been judged a devilish human being carries out his father's order and thereby shows himself to be an obedient and dutiful son. Sokel suggests that this obedience itself is subversive: "Georg contradicts his father—this is the story's final paradox—by obeying him."[49] It is Georg who has the final say: the hermeneutical tyrant's interpretation has been resisted, but the price has been Georg's life.

The battle between father and son ends with the father's condemnation of his son and the son's acceptance of that verdict, but then a transformation in the son occurs by which he regains some measure of agency, a voice by which to refute the father's verdict through words of love.[50] Georg declares his love for his parents in a voice devoid of the self-deception that marked him in the opening scene and of the fear and vigilance that characterized his conversation with his father. And yet along with the love for his parents, there is also a refutation or resistance of the father's hermeneutical tyranny, of his simple and reductive declaration, in Georg's expression of love.

The last line of the story suggests the strong connections between love, power, sexuality, and death: "In diesem Augenblick ging über die Brücke ein geradezu unendlicher Verkehr." As Georg lets himself drop from the bridge, an "unending stream of traffic was just going over the bridge" (88). The word Kafka uses for traffic (*Verkehr*) is also the word for sexual intercourse. Max Brod quotes Kafka as saying, "Do you know what the last sentence [of "The Judgment"] means? When I wrote it, I had in mind a violent ejaculation."[51] The phrase "violent ejaculation" draws a connection between sexual pleasure and violence. The fact that Kafka had it in mind as his protagonist plunges to his death furthers the connection between sexuality, power, and death that has characterized his conversation with his father.

Butler offers the evocative suggestion that the last line of the story, which seems to come from a consciousness other than Georg's, "may be the voice of the imaginary friend to whom both Georg and his father were said to have written, and it may be that this friend turns out to have been writing the two of them, transitively, all along."[52] Butler does not, however, push this line of thinking further to propose that Kafka himself is the friend, the imaginary friend who has written father and son and who has been written by them, the author as friend of his characters. In an extraordinary inversion of our usual understanding of the relation between author and characters, we discover Kafka the writer as a character imagined and written by the other characters in the text: Georg and his father imagine Kafka as the friend to whom they have written—the one who has "gone off the tracks," who is "wild and alone"—and whom they have written. They have written to him before he writes them, and we learn of him through their battle over whose letters have had the power to render him a reader, whose letters he has been convinced or enticed to read. Kafka the writer of "The Judgment" becomes Kafka the friend, who is constituted by the accounts of his characters as the one who reads their writings and survives their deaths or collapses and thus can then voice their story. Butler goes on to describe the voice that speaks the final line of the story. The voice we hear, she suggests, is a

> voice that belongs to no one and whose proximity to the event is logically impossible, is purely fictive, perhaps the sublimity of fiction itself. Although the story narrates a death, it also preserves a voice in the final narrative line, suggesting that a human something survives, that narration has some propitious relation to survival. What remains peculiar, however, is that this is a written voice with no body and no name, a voice extracted from the scene of address itself, one whose extraction, paradoxically, forms the basis of survival. The voice is ghostly, impossible, disembodied, and yet it persists, living on.[53]

Does this not sound like a fantasy Kafka might have imagined for his own survival in the world: "a written voice with no body and no name"?

Kafka suggests the hermeneutical complexity of his story when he writes to Felice,

> But you don't even know your little story ["The Judgment"] yet. It is somewhat wild and meaningless and if it didn't express some inner truth (which can never be universally established, but has to be accepted or denied every time by each reader or listener in turn), it would be nothing.[54]

True to his tendency to compress many different strands of thought into so few words, Kafka presents the following possibilities as to how his story can be interpreted: the story can express an inner truth or it can be nothing (either way it is "somewhat wild and meaningless"). If it expresses an inner truth, it is one that cannot be universally established once and for all. Instead, it is an inner truth that has to be accepted or denied by each reader or listener. Thus, we are left with the following choice: the story is nothing or it expresses an inner truth that each reader can deny or accept but that cannot be universally established. What is affirmed is that the story is *somewhat* wild and meaningless. What is ruled out is that the story can express a universally established truth.

Kafka's commentary raises several questions: How can the story be somewhat meaningless and have an inner truth at the same time? What would it mean for a reader to deny the inner truth of the story—or, for that matter, accept it? What does it mean for a story to be nothing? At issue, then, are first, *the nature of the story* (it expresses an inner truth or it is nothing); second, *the nature of the reader's response* to the story (the reader accepts or denies the inner truth expressed in the story, if it is determined that indeed one is therein expressed); and, finally, *the nature of the story's "truth"* (an inner truth, not universally established, and yet one that is accepted or denied by each reader each time the story is read).

Kafka's insistence on the role of each reader in affirming or denying the truth of the story indicates the importance he places on individual views and perspectives and his resistance to the idea of a truth that can be grasped once and for all. Truth, for Kafka, does not take the form of propositions, or any other static form; rather, as he writes to Milena in a letter, "it's difficult to tell the truth, since there is only one truth, but that truth is alive and therefore has a lively, changing face."[55] Truth is something we engage like a face, like a person, drawing near, expecting change—a living thing rather than a static object. Because of this, interpretation itself cannot take the form of mere decipherment, like solving a puzzle or decoding a message. What is necessary is the ongoing interaction between story and readers, ongoing interpretive activity—interpretation that does not find an end in completion or in abandonment of the task because of despair. Kafka's resistance to a universal truth does not render the story completely meaningless, nor does it suggest a relativistic view of truth. There is, as he says to Milena, only one truth, but it is alive. It is, rather, the reader's response to the inner truth of the story that is relative—relative to each reader—and it is the reader who decides whether to accept or deny the story's truth. This understanding of interpretation in response to the story is a far cry from the power of interpretation in the story, where interpretations have the power of death sentences. Instead, the reader's interpretive activity claims no mastery nor to have found *the* meaning of the text. A much more modest yet no less important task is assigned to the reader: to accept or deny some inner truth each time she reads the story—perhaps a different inner meaning each time.

The hermeneutical tyrant asserts his proclamations as universally established truths, and the impotent subject submits to the interpretations of the tyrant out of fear or powerlessness. In contrast, Kafka outlines a relationship between text and reader that resists both tyranny and despair. Kafka's construction of the relationship between text and reader supports the integrity of the text and the freedom of the reader without reducing either—without reducing, on the one hand, the truth of the text to the reader's interpretation of it or, on the other, the role of the reader to one who must find the universal truth of the text.

The story reveals the dangers of interpretation in the battle for power between father and son and depicts the destructive consequences of definitive interpretation and subjection to it. And yet, according to Kafka, it also offers the reader an opportunity to resist these two modes of interpretation through ongoing interpretive engagement with the text and the changing face of its inner truth. Kafka said of "The Judgment," "It is also my favorite work and so I always wished for it to be appreciated if possible by itself."[56] Although Georg's resistance to hermeneutical tyranny costs him his life, Kafka's reader can resist hermeneutical tyranny by engaging in the ongoing interpretive activity that the story seeks to elicit, denying or affirming its inner truth each time she reads the story and thereby appreciating it "by itself" as Kafka wished.

Chapter 3

✦

The Virtue of Hesitation and the Temptation of Resolution

Kafka's "The Metamorphosis" and Todorov's Fantastic

Thus far in the book I have explored, in the first chapter, the different modes of interpretation Kafka describes in his "Letter to His Father" and the fantasy of complete interpretation that tempts many of us, and, in the second chapter, the accumulation of different forms of capital and the exercise of power as a means to control the interpretive realm itself. In this chapter, I look more closely at the interpretive categories we use to make sense of the world around us when that world is not amenable to ready comprehension. What happens when we are confronted by something that falls outside of, or does not fit, our categories?

Gregor Samsa is just such a "text." By now, his strange metamorphosis into a monstrous vermin has become rather familiar to readers of European literature. The description of the initial scene—a man awakes one morning to find himself transformed into a giant bug—typically arouses recognition rather than surprise. Though familiarity has numbed us to the shock of Gregor's transformation, it has in no way impeded our fascination with the story, as the sheer mass of writing about it indicates. Kafka's "The Metamorphosis" arouses and sustains its readers' interpretive drives. Scholars are highly conscious of the power the story has to elicit interpretation—very few works written on it fail to mention the quantity of critical response to the story. In fact, the interpretive activity Kafka's story elicits has become a subject of interpretation itself.

As I have been arguing, Kafka's works do more than *elicit* interpretation: they are also works *about* interpretation. They depict characters confronting events, situations, and people that call for and frustrate those characters' interpretive activity. By examining the interpretive activities *in*

Kafka's story—that is, the characters' responses to Gregor's inscrutable metamorphosis—and the interpretive activities *about* Kafka's story—his readers' responses to the inscrutable story "The Metamorphosis"—we can begin to understand the landscape of interpretive activity Kafka's writing maps out.

In "The Metamorphosis," both the characters and the reader experience the need to interpret in situations in which it is very difficult to do so; their interpretive categories simply do not have the capacity to make sense of what is before them. The characters confront something (Gregor's metamorphosis) that disrupts their interpretive framework and yet calls for interpretation nonetheless. Likewise, the reader confronts something (Kafka's story) that disrupts her interpretive framework, does not fit the categories with which she usually interprets texts, and yet calls for interpretation nonetheless. In each case, the confrontation with a metamorphosis/"Metamorphosis" radically challenges interpretive categories and practices, creating a tension between the need to interpret and the difficulty of doing so.

The range of ways that readers and characters respond to this tension sketches the outlines of a landscape of interpretation. In the end, Gregor's family resolves the tension that Gregor's metamorphosis creates by "forgetting" his humanity and declaring him to be not Gregor but a vermin, thus seeming to resolve the ambiguity of his new identity and justifying his expulsion from the family and his death. The characters ignore the aspects of Gregor's identity that disrupt their interpretive categories in order to arrive at a seemingly self-evident interpretation in a move that displays the tyranny of simplicity. Rather than celebrating the creativity of misreading (à la Harold Bloom's theory of the anxiety of influence), "The Metamorphosis," I argue, articulates the range of misreading's destructive possibilities, its implicit endorsement of totalizing interpretations of what is other, and its erasure of what does not fit into our interpretive categories. The reader is challenged not to follow in the Samsa family's footsteps but instead to resist the temptation to simplify the story or Gregor so that either fits neatly into her interpretive framework.

After examining the ways in which Gregor and his family interpret his identity after the metamorphosis, I look at how one critic, Tzvetan Todorov, interprets "The Metamorphosis," showing how even so insightful a reader of literature as he finds it difficult to resist the temptation to resolve ambiguity. Todorov's theory of the fantastic and, in particular, his application of it to Kafka's story provide a way to think about the reader's position before the Kafkan text. Todorov's articulation of the specific hesitation the reader experiences between two ways of interpreting the events of a fantastic story—as real and thus uncanny, on the one hand, or as unreal and thus marvelous, on the other—points to the general hermeneutical hesitation the reader experiences when faced with a story like "The Metamorphosis." The fact that his family's resolution of hesitation *in the story* leads to Gregor's death suggests that the stakes may also be high in the resolution of hesitation *in response to the story* and serves to warn the reader against taking such a path. In fact, Kafka's story suggests that there are situations in which the resolution of hesitation is morally culpable, erases complexity in order to arrive at the fantasy of complete interpretation, and may do violence when what is being interpreted is a living being rather than a text.

Hesitation, then, marks the willingness to keep open two opposing options; it reveals the recognition that both point to something true about the text even when they seem to be at odds or even contradictory. Therefore hesitation does not have a negative valence here—it is not about indecision due to a lack of willpower, uncertainty due to weak apprehension, or a will divided between conflicting desires. Rather, it indicates the position of remaining in tension between two possible interpretations and resisting the temptation to opt for one over the other by ignoring, forgetting, repressing, or erasing aspects of the text that trouble such a decision.

Despite inconsistencies in Todorov's descriptions of the traditional fantastic, which depend on whether he is trying to distinguish it from the uncanny and the marvelous or from Kafka's works, Todorov brings out an important aspect of "The Metamorphosis" by looking at it in the context of the fantastic: the hermeneutical hesitation it brings about, and sustains, in the reader. Herein lies one aspect of the effect Kafka's works have on their reader: they confront her with something that calls for ongoing interpretation and yet, at the same time, cannot be definitively interpreted. The result is that she has to revise her understanding of the activity of interpretation, finding a richer range of ways to engage Kafka's texts than simply deciphering their meaning as one would solve a puzzle. This involves a willingness to hesitate, to pause, to resist the immediacy of closure and the pleasures of completion.

Gregor's Shocking Failure to Interpret the Shocking Event

Gregor Samsa's response to having "found himself changed in his bed into a monstrous vermin"[1] is perhaps even more shocking than the metamorphosis itself. Though he initially asks, "What's happened to me?" (3), he is easily distracted from this question by the rainy weather. It is the overcast sky, rather than his domelike brown belly, that "completely depresse[s] him" (3). In fact, he is more concerned with getting to the office than with figuring out what has happened to him. He cannot get back to sleep, despite his desire to do so, not because of his horror at his new form but because he cannot quite manage to get himself over onto his right side, the position in which he usually sleeps. Gregor's mundane response to his metamorphosis reveals the gap between the response the reader might expect a character to have to such a transformation and the one Gregor actually does have, which builds tension between the reader's perspective and the narrative point of view that presents his metamorphosis.

The mundane nature of the details given and of Gregor's concerns is so incommensurate with the alarming nature of the metamorphosis that they strike the reader as absurdly out of place. (They also make the opening to "The Metamorphosis" initially quite funny, though this aspect of the story has been missed by many readers.) Instead of bewailing his present condition, which the reader reasonably expects Gregor to do, he begins to moan about his job: "Oh God. . . . What a grueling job I've picked" (3). In what might be one of literature's greatest understatements, Gregor decides that he is not feeling "especially fresh" (4). Gregor is more concerned with his inability to get to work, and the inquiries that this has elicited from his family and the office manager, who arrives to check on his tardiness, than he is about the fact that he has been transformed into a giant insect. These narrative details provide a startling contrast to the momentousness of the event that has just transpired. In fact, as Todorov suggests, "the most surprising thing is precisely the absence of surprise with regard to the unheard-of event that has befallen Gregor Samsa . . . ('We shall never be sufficiently amazed about this lack of amazement,' Camus once said apropos of Kafka)."[2]

Todorov argues that the narrative movement of "The Metamorphosis" is a naturalizing one in which what initially appears to be a supernatural event becomes increasingly naturalized. However, no character, including Gregor himself, seems to find his transformation a supernatural event. No character ever thinks or says, "But this is impossible—how can a man become a bug?" Michael Wood suggests that this lack of surprise is characteristic of many of Kafka's characters: "Kafka's characters seek to domesticate surprise, to refuse the extraordinariness of the extraordinary."[3] Gregor asks himself "What has happened to me?" as one might ask oneself about a suddenly sore back, and quickly moves on. Contrary to Todorov's reading, it is not the case that Gregor "at first thinks he is dreaming; but is quickly convinced of the contrary."[4] He knows at once that it is "no dream" (3). And also contrary to Todorov's reading, it is not the case that Gregor "does not immediately *stop* seeking a rational explanation;"[5] he never *begins* to look for one. He takes his metamorphosis as a given, though a rather inconvenient one; the problem he faces is not his metamorphosis but how to get to work and avoid or mitigate the negative impact his lateness has caused in the family and at work. What for the reader seems an impossible event is for Gregor most pressingly an inconvenient hindrance to getting to work on time. Thus it is not, as Todorov argues, "gradually" that "Gregor accepts his situation as unusual but, after all, possible";[6] rather, from the very beginning it has been for him possible and actual. Gregor's metamorphosis is not a "shocking, impossible event which . . . *ends* by becoming possible, paradoxically enough";[7] throughout the story, the characters consistently view Gregor's metamorphosis as a possible and actual, though inconvenient or disturbing, event.

The Reader's Hermeneutical Hesitation

It is for the reader that the metamorphosis is both possible and impossible. She wonders whether Gregor is dreaming, whether this is a figurative description of his state, or whether this story takes place in a marvelous world in which things like this happen as a matter of course. That is, the reader attempts to understand how a seemingly impossible event has taken place. These hypotheses—that Gregor is dreaming, that what she has read so far is a figurative description of his state, or that this is a marvelous world—are refuted by narrative details in the story; it is not a dream or a delusion. An impossible event seems really to have happened.

This is precisely the nature of the "generalized fantastic" as Todorov defines it: "The Kafkaesque narrative abandons . . . the hesitation represented within the text"—that is, the hesitation before the choice of interpreting the event as real or imaginary, possible or impossible.[8] Even though Todorov seems to misread Gregor's initial reaction to his metamorphosis, he rightly argues that "the supernatural is given, and yet it does not cease to seem inadmissible *to us*."[9] For the characters do not deny that such a metamorphosis is possible, whereas the reader cannot decide between its possibility and impossibility. The power of the story is in part constituted by the tension between the ways the characters and the readers interpret Gregor's metamorphosis.

This tension lies not merely in the fact that the characters do not ask *how* Gregor's metamorphosis is possible but also in that they do not try to understand *why* it has happened once they have discovered *that* it has happened. James Rolleston, in describing the typical Kafkan protagonist, points out that he "ignores, misunderstands, or represses a truth that the reader sees and must respond to."[10] In Gregor's case, he seems to ignore the momentousness of his metamorphosis and to have no interest in discovering its cause or meaning. He treats his metamorphosis as if it were "nonsense" (3), merely "today's fantasy" (6), a temporary inconvenience, similar to a cold: "That the change in his voice was nothing more than the first sign of a bad cold, an occupational ailment of the traveling salesman, he had no doubt in the least" (6). As if assigning the cause of his transformation to a lack of sleep, he says to himself, "This getting up so early . . . makes anyone a complete idiot. Human beings have to have their sleep" (4). Gregor continues this way of thinking of his transformation as merely an uncomfortable and temporary inconvenience when he considers, with some pleasure, that one "really had to grant the possibility" (8) that the office manager could someday wake up in the same predicament, as if wishing a bad case of arthritis on him. Gregor appears to be a bad reader of events; he fails to interpret his metamorphosis by misreading it as merely a temporary problem. This gap between the event of Gregor's metamorphosis and his response to it, as Rolleston points out, creates a kind of unease in the reader that she herself cannot quite interpret: "A basic discrepancy in the hero's view of himself is felt by the reader from the outset . . . [though she is] aware that the hero is wrong, the reader cannot say what is right."[11]

Gregor's failure to interpret his new state only adds to the hermeneutical burden of the reader as she attempts to understand why Gregor has become a bug, as well as why he seems so uninterested in this question. David Eggenschwiler points out that "because the humdrum world that Gregor inhabits is not an appropriate setting for such nocturnal metamorphoses, we (if not the characters) cast about for an explanation."[12] Gregor's lack of response seems strange because it is not how a person would normally be expected to respond to some sort of radical transformation.

Gregor's concerns with the mundane details of his life remind us of his humanity, while the numerous physical details of his new body prevent us from forgetting his "verminality." Is Gregor vermin or human? The answer to that question provides the basis for interpreting his thoughts and actions, and yet it is precisely that question that the reader and characters cannot answer. He is both and neither. The reader's and the characters' ability to interpret Gregor's transformation, to understand what it means and why it has happened, are undermined by the fact that there is no category for a human/vermin. Gregor's ontological status causes a breakdown of interpretive categories, bringing tension and hermeneutical insecurity. Gregor's transformation calls for a transformation of the reader's and the characters' interpretive categories—new categories will be needed to understand his new identity, and even they may not be adequate to a complete fulfillment of the task.

The reader confronts the temptation to resolve the tension that Gregor's new identity arouses and to arrive at reasons for his metamorphosis, explanations for his lack of interest in interpreting it, and a definition of the being that he presently is. However, the text resists these resolutions while still calling the reader to continue in her interpretive enterprise. For the reader is unable to read Gregor's metamorphosis with the passivity and indifference with which he seems to respond to it: it is too shocking an event.

The Family's Interpretive Activity—Before and After

The reader seeks to understand what has happened to Gregor; Gregor does not. He is unable or unwilling to interpret his own situation, or even to attempt to interpret it; rather, he seeks his cue from others' interpretations of him.

> If they were shocked, then Gregor had no further responsibility and could be calm. But if they took everything calmly, then he, too, had no reason to get excited, and could, if he hurried, actually be at the station by eight o'clock. (10)

His response to his metamorphosis will, he decides, be determined by the response of his family and the office manager. Whatever their response, he can be calm because either he has no responsibility for such a shocking transformation or, if they are calm, then there is no reason for him not to be calm as well. The fact that the others "no longer understood his words" (11) suggests that Gregor may indeed be freed from responsibility, because this means that they cannot possibly expect him to have an explanation for his metamorphosis. Someone who is unable to speak cannot be expected to explain.

Before Gregor emerges from the room, there is quite a bit of interest in exactly what is going on behind those locked doors. The father asks Gregor, "What's going on?" (5). Grete asks, "Is something the matter with you?" (5). His mother tells the manager that "there's certainly something wrong with him" (8–9). The manager asks for "an immediate, clear explanation" (9). Even though there is still time for Gregor to make the eight o'clock train, suggesting that he is only a few hours late for work, the office manager has already made the journey to his house to investigate Gregor's not showing up at work.

And yet at the sight of him, the desire for explanations vanishes. The office manager and Gregor's family are quite intent on getting an explanation for why Gregor is late for work, but after catching sight of him they make no attempt to find an explanation for his metamorphosis, an event that calls much more urgently for interpretation. They refuse to entertain the seemingly obvious questions of why and how it has happened and what it could mean.

Instead of asking for an explanation for what has happened to Gregor, the office manager backs away slowly "as if there were some secret prohibition against leaving the room" (13). He then flees with haste as soon as he is out of the living room, reaching out toward the staircase "as if nothing less than an unearthly deliverance were awaiting him there" (13). The sense of religious taboo and yearning for salvation are thereby referenced in the same movement away from Gregor. The office manager's horrified retreat is not a surprising response to the advance of a giant bug, but the fact that he never returns, even though he has left his hat, coat, and cane, and that no communication ever comes from the office again seems rather odd—especially since, by Gregor's account, the company is vigilant in its watch over him. It is "a firm where at the slightest omission they immediately suspected the worst" (7). In fact, when Gregor was still lying in bed, he realized that

> the messenger boy had been waiting at the five o'clock train and would have long ago reported his not showing up. . . . What if he were to say he was sick? . . . The boss himself would be sure to come with the health-insurance doctor, blame his parents for their lazy son, and cut off all excuses by quoting the health-insurance doctor, for whom the world consisted of people who were completely healthy but afraid to work. (4–5)

And yet, after Gregor's metamorphosis and the manager's departure, the boss and the health-insurance doctor never come to check on him, nor does the family receive any communication whatsoever from the company. The office that has sent the manager to investigate why Gregor is a few hours late for work shows no interest in investigating why he never again shows up at the office, even though there is also the issue of the debt to the company that Gregor is working to pay off for the family. Even if the company simply considers Gregor retired or fired, surely a debt that would take Gregor "five or six years" (4) more of work to pay off is not one they would neglect. Nonetheless, as Walter Sokel astutely points out, "it seems that Gregor's *Schreckgestalt*, his new terrifying shape, which the first morning after his awakening had chased away the deputy of the firm, has thereby also canceled the parents' debt."[13]

It is, in fact, the preponderance of hermeneutical activity and attention surrounding Gregor's "late start" that makes it so striking that no explanation for Gregor's metamorphosis itself is sought. Just as Gregor's avoidance of interpreting his metamorphosis arouses the reader's suspicion, so, too, does the family's and office manager's insistence on procuring an explanation for a relatively minor event—being late for work. The reader wonders why there is such attention focused on his lateness, since there are several easy explanations ready at hand for being late, such as oversleeping, coming down with a cold, or, less likely but possible, being called away on unexpected family business. Gregor's avoidance of interpretation and the other characters' obsession with interpretation arouse the reader's suspicion for precisely the same reason—the disjunction between the amount of interpretation an event seems to warrant and the amount it elicits. While Gregor barely interprets an event that calls for interpretation, the family and office manager are obsessed with interpreting an event that barely seems to merit any.

Upon seeing Gregor's metamorphosed body, the family and the manager desist from any hermeneutical attempts to understand what has happened. It is not simply that Gregor's metamorphosis serves as an explanation for why he is late and, thus, the other characters have received the explanation they sought. Rather, Gregor's metamorphosis renders their inquiry about his tardiness superfluous and ridiculous. The appearance of Gregor's verminous form shatters their desire for an explanation.[14] The reason for this might be that Gregor the traveling salesman and family breadwinner, who has overslept and missed his train, seems to be a safe "text" to interpret, but Gregor the monstrous vermin is not. Through his metamorphosis, Gregor becomes an unreadable text, one that resists definitive interpretation and disrupts the hermeneutical drive.[15] His metamorphosis brings to an end the microscopic investigations and scrutiny of his employers and family.

The Displacement of the Hermeneutical

Gregor's emergence from the room not only puts an end to all requests for an explanation but also seems to disrupt the very ability of the characters to speak. Gregor's voice is described as "the voice of an animal" (10). The other characters seem to mirror this aspect of Gregor's metamorphosis. The office manager's words are reduced to "Agh!" (14) as he flees. His father hesitates between a voiceless violence and sorrow: he first forms a fist "with a hostile expression" on his face (12), then begins to weep, and then stamps his feet and waves a walking stick in one hand and a newspaper in the other. The father no longer speaks but makes an "intolerable hissing sound" (15). In fact the father's voice is so transformed that to Gregor it does "not sound like that of only a single father" (15), suggesting the expansion of his voice to that of an army of fathers. In Kafka's "Letter to His Father" and "The Judgment" the fathers appear as giants—enormous versions of themselves—but here the father's voice seems multiplied into a hostile chorus of fathers' voices. Although the father's hissing noises and utterance of "Shoo!" are not uncommon exclamations to seeing a large bug in one's house, Gregor interprets them as savage, somehow other than human. The section ends with the cessation of all language: "And then at last everything was quiet" (15). The flurry of questions and demands for explanation ceases at Gregor's appearance, and language no longer seems adequate to engage with the metamorphosis before them.

This silence continues into the next section of the story: "While at this hour of the day his father was in the habit of reading the afternoon newspaper in a loud voice to his mother and sometimes to his sister too, now there wasn't a sound" (16). Reading, interpretation, and language have stopped. The shattering of the family's hermeneutic desire and linguistic abilities caused by Gregor's metamorphosis is symbolized in the relation of the family to the newspaper. When the father is initially trying to shoo Gregor away, he waves a "heavy newspaper" (14) in one hand—note the unusually enlarged status of the newspaper as somehow "heavy." Then the sheets of the newspaper flutter in disarray across the floor, rustled by the wind coming from outside, reflecting the scattering of the family's hermeneutical desire. The family's main activities before the metamorphosis had centered around the reading of newspapers: the father sat at the breakfast table "for hours while reading various newspapers" (12) as his daily morning routine, the afternoon was spent with the father reading the paper to his wife and daughter, and one might surmise that Gregor was joined in the evening as he sat "quietly reading the paper" (8). After the metamorphosis, there is no mention of family newspaper reading, little conversation of any sort, and no attempt at interpreting this odd catastrophe that has befallen them. The family's activities shift from reading and interpreting to doing and working, from hermeneutical activity to physical activity.

Gregor's relation to newspapers after his metamorphosis repeats the shift from the realm of the linguistic to the physical that his family's relation to it undergoes. The newspaper that had so often been the center of family community becomes the weapon whereby his father chases him away from the family and back into his room. Gregor gets no "news directly" (19) (except from the newspaper under his food, and then it is old news, or when it is struck against his back, and then it is bad news). That the newspaper becomes the serving tray for his food symbolizes the subservience of the linguistic realm to the bodily realm. Faced with a text that is uninterpretable according to their usual methods and categories of interpretation, Gregor's family avoids the realm of interpretation altogether, rather than seeking a new way to engage in it.

Even in Gregor's daily movements, this shift from the linguistic to the physical occurs. Like his family's avoidance of thinking about Gregor's metamorphosis by engaging in nonlinguistic activities, Gregor avoids thinking about it by distracting himself through movement: "In order not to get involved in such thoughts, Gregor decided to keep moving, and he crawled up and down the room" (16). Gregor moves in order to avoid the task of interpreting his metamorphosis; his family members throw themselves into working and refrain from talking also to avoid the seemingly uninterpretable text in their midst.

Misreading Family

Though his metamorphosis dispels the interpretive activity of his family and fails to elicit it in him, Gregor does engage in acts of interpretation after his metamorphosis (though not interpretation *of* his metamorphosis)—he interprets the actions of others. His hermeneutical activity is directed toward his family, particularly his sister, Grete, rather than himself. He carefully interprets Grete's actions so as to preserve the illusion that she feels kindly toward him and that their intimate relationship has not been broken. For example, he interprets her quick withdrawal from the room as issuing from her desire to let him know that "he might make himself as comfortable as he wanted" (18) in eating the food she leaves, rather than from any fear or repulsion on her part. It is not so important to Gregor that her actions *are* kind but that he is able to interpret them as such: "Gregor sometimes caught a remark which was meant to be friendly *or could be interpreted as such*" (19; emphasis mine). Gregor seems more interested in preserving his interpretation, his illusion of intimacy with Grete, than in examining what her actions suggest.

Grete is the one person with whom Gregor had a close personal connection before his metamorphosis; though he provided financial support to his parents, "no special feeling of warmth went with it anymore. Only his sister had remained close to Gregor" (20). His lonely life as a traveling salesman left him no time for a real social life. Romantic relationships were limited to brief sexual encounters with maids and cashiers. He spent his evenings at home reading newspapers and railway timetables. Most recently, he had carved a picture frame in which he had placed an illustration from a magazine of a woman wrapped in fur. For a character who "has nothing on his mind but the business . . . never goes out nights" (8), locks all three of his bedroom doors, and has as his wall decoration not a picture of family, friends, or girlfriend but a magazine illustration of a fur-covered model, the intimate relationship he has with his sister is unique.

The idea that his sister's remarks might not be kindly meant is too unsettling for Gregor to accept. Consequently, he resorts to misreading—forgetting part of the "text" of her remarks in order to interpret them in a more comforting way. Initially he had tried to forget his metamorphosis by going back to sleep: "How about going back to sleep for a few minutes and forgetting all this nonsense" (3). Likewise, when the family's business collapsed, his "sole concern had been to do everything in his power to make the family forget as quickly as possible the business disaster which had plunged everyone into a state of total despair" (20). His family shares with Gregor this trait of wanting to forget misfortune as soon as it happens. His mother does not want to remove the furniture from Gregor's room "so that when Gregor comes back to us again, he'll find everything unchanged and can forget all the more easily what's happened in the meantime" (24). Her emphasis is on enabling Gregor to forget his metamorphosis once it is over, just as Gregor's emphasis had been on enabling his parents to forget the financial disaster that befell the family business as soon as possible.

Grete also exhibits this family trait. Before Gregor's metamorphosis, she was "a little useless" (23), but now she is deeply appreciated for taking care of Gregor and thus enabling her parents to avoid direct contact with him: "During the first two weeks, his parents could not bring themselves to come in to him, and often he heard them say how much they appreciated his sister's work" (23). Grete thus takes over Gregor's role of helping their parents avoid facing their misfortune. Just as Gregor had thrown himself into his work in order to help his family forget their first catastrophe, so Grete takes on the duties of caring for Gregor so that her parents can, if not forget the second, then at least avoid direct contact with this second catastrophe. In each case, the child takes on the role of shielding the parents from the disturbance of a catastrophe that has economic, social, and psychological consequences for them. The parents are enabled in their misreading by being shielded from those elements of the catastrophe that might disturb comfortable readings. The end of the story continues both the family trait of "forgetting" misfortune in order to overcome it—in this case forgetting that the monstrous vermin in their midst is a family member—and the parents' dependence on their children when they pin their hopes for the future on Grete, for whom they will find a husband.

Literary theorist Wolfgang Iser argues that "the act of interpretation . . . is a basic element of the reading process" and that as the individual reads a text, he or she "will continually strive, even if unconsciously, to fit everything together in a consistent pattern."[16] In the process, the reader uncovers "impulses which cannot be immediately integrated or will even resist final integration."[17] He "is forced to discover hitherto unconscious expectations that underlie all his perceptions, and also the whole process of consistency-building as a prerequisite for understanding. In this way he may then be given the chance of discovering himself, both in and through his constant involvement in 'home-made' illusions and fictions."[18] Not every reader takes up this opportunity to discover himself through a recognition and exploration of the illusions and fictions with which he interprets. But slowly we begin to see a process like this unfold in Gregor: he comes to realize that he has been trying to fit together the details of Grete's entrances into his room in such a way as to preserve the illusion that she feels only kindly toward him. He finally understands "that the sight of him [is] still repulsive to [Grete] and [is] bound to remain repulsive to her in the future" (22). The one person with whom he had remained intimate after becoming a traveling salesman is repulsed by his new physical appearance, a fact that does not fit into Gregor's narrative of the kind, loyal sister. He faces the fact that "he ha[s] had to ignore so much of the potential content of the text [in this case, Grete's actions toward him] in order to formulate his restricted interpretation."[19] In realizing this, Gregor reveals that he is becoming a better reader, able to see beyond his own interpretive strategies: the text tells us that "in time Gregor, too, saw things much more clearly" (22).

However, Gregor's response to this insight is to shield his sister from what disturbs her about the text his metamorphosed body constitutes, thus continuing his role of helping his family avoid and forget their misfortunes. Becoming a better reader leads him to encourage misreading by his sister. Gregor covers the sofa with a sheet so that Grete will not have to see him, foreshadowing his death at the end of the story, in which he "disappears" so that his family will no longer be burdened by his presence among them. His acceptance of the fact that she cannot live with the sight of him and his willingness to remove himself from view begin the process whereby he will accept the fact that the family cannot live with him at all, and then he will remove himself completely from their midst.

Gregor's Struggle to Retain His Humanity

At this point in the story, Gregor still hopes to maintain his humanity and his connection with the human world and his past, even if it is mediated by the covering of a sheet. The scene in which his mother and sister begin to take furniture out of his room shows what a complicated matter this is. For Gregor's animal and human instincts exist in tension in his consciousness. The question he poses to himself, a question he cannot easily answer, reveals the conflict in his desires:

> Had he really wanted to have his warm room, comfortably fitted with furniture that had always been in the family, changed into a cave, in which, of course, he would be able to crawl around unhampered in all directions but at the cost of simultaneously, rapidly, and totally forgetting his human past? (25)

It is his mother's voice that draws him back from the "verge of forgetting" (25). His connection with his human identity and past has begun to weaken, and he has begun to take pleasure in the particularities of his new form: "He especially liked hanging from the ceiling . . . in the almost happy absent-mindedness which Gregor felt up there" (24). Hearing the voice of his mother, however, Gregor realizes that "the fact that not a soul had addressed a word directly to him, must have addled his brain in the course of the last two months" (24). Here it is made explicit that language and the human voice are Gregor's link with humanity, but because of this, his attempts to maintain his human connection are nearly impossible.

For Gregor is unable to speak to his family. They are unable to understand the sounds he utters, which to him are words with meaning, and they do not realize that he can understand the words they say. Only the reader is aware of any linguistic, interpretive activity on Gregor's part. Only the reader is privy to Gregor's thoughts and thereby can recognize his humanness. Later in the story Gregor's father moans, "If he could understand us" (38). The reader might respond, "If only they knew that he *can* understand them!" For if the family knew that Gregor could understand them and if Gregor could somehow communicate with them, this story might have a very different ending. His parents and sister are functionally deaf to Gregor, and he is functionally mute to them, whereas they think he is deaf to their words and so they remain mute toward him. The ties connecting Gregor to his family, a family prone to forgetting whatever reminds them of unfortunate events, become very tenuous without communication and mutual understanding.

Because of this failure of language, the physical objects that connect Gregor to the time before his metamorphosis, to the time when he was part of the family and fully a member of humanity, take on extreme importance for him. Though the removal of furniture from his room would provide him with more space, it would be "at the cost of . . . totally forgetting his human past" (25). Significantly, it is the writing desk that Gregor decides he cannot do without, that must stay. The desk serves both as a reminder of his human past—it was the writing desk that "he had done his homework on when he was a student at business college, in high school, yes, even in public school" (26)—and as a connection to the linguistic realm, to the time when he was able to make himself understood through language. Unlike the "bad" reader who wants to forget those things that complicate the formulation of an interpretation, Gregor decides he wants to retain his link with humanity and, by doing so, retain his ambiguous and complicated identity as both human and vermin. In this instance, Gregor resists the temptation to forget what troubles definitive interpretation. By clinging to what reminds him of his humanity, Gregor resists becoming unambiguously a bug and so resists becoming what can be unambiguously interpreted.

His mother's voice reminds him of his humanity, but when his sister and mother are silent, Gregor begins to forget about them and his humanity: "He had no more time to examine the good intentions of the two women, whose existence, besides, he had almost forgotten, for they were so exhausted that they were working in silence, and one could hear only the heavy shuffling of their feet" (26). Gregor no longer thinks of them in their relation to him, as his family members, and these "two women," as he now refers to them, whom he had once shielded from misfortune, are replaced in their importance by "the picture of the lady all dressed in fur" (26). Now it is the animal-like woman whom Gregor shields from the misfortune of being taken from him, by pressing his hot belly upon the cool glass surface and completely covering her. Gregor behaves like a dog jealously guarding a bone. His sister, whom he later imagines keeping in his room and protecting by spitting at any intruders, is now herself the intruder trying to take away his fur lady. Gregor's imagined response to her intrusion is, "Well, just let her try! He squatted on his picture and would not give it up. He would rather fly in Grete's face" (26).[20]

The narcissistic imagery here is obvious. The picture of the woman in the fur, her humanity hidden by animalistic covering, hangs on the wall like a mirror revealing to Gregor a transformation parallel to his own—the woman's forearm vanishes into a fur muff rendering her identity ambiguously located between human and animal. Taken out of a magazine, captured in a frame, and secluded in the privacy of Gregor's locked bedroom, she becomes a text only for Gregor, just as Gregor's metamorphosis relegates him to the seclusion of his bedroom and renders him an unreadable text for the rest of the family. The frame, like the walls of the bedroom, serves to intensify and isolate its contents. Both the lady in fur and Gregor are characterized by, first, a metamorphosis that results in an ambiguous identity; second, isolation from the social sphere and relegation to the private sphere; third, objectification, in the sense of becoming an object of speculation rather than a partner in conversation; and, finally, frustrated efforts at human connection—the lady holds out to the viewer her arm, which has disappeared inside the fur muff, a gesture that can never be reciprocated, and Gregor's attempts to reach out to his family are continually misunderstood and thus not reciprocated either.

It is worth noting that Gregor's mother fails to mention the picture of the lady in fur when she tells the office manager about the picture frame Gregor made to put it in: "In the span of two or three evenings he carved a little frame. You'll be amazed how pretty it is; it's hanging in his room. You'll see it right away when Gregor opens the door" (8). This omission of the fur lady and, one might say, of the erotic motivation of Gregor's "artwork," this reduction of it from an erotic image in a frame to simply the frame itself, foreshadows other omissions and reductions his mother makes as she attempts to avoid the disruptive elements of Gregor's metamorphosis. Conversely, Gregor never thinks about the frame or his making of it. His investment in the picture does not have to do with the time he spent making the frame; rather, the time he spent making the frame reveals his investment in the picture. Further, his lack of thinking about the frame may indicate an effort to avoid thinking about the desires for possession the frame suggests: with the frame, he has framed/captured the fur lady, just as he later fantasizes about capturing Grete.

Significantly, when Gregor's mother sees him next, it is as a "gigantic brown blotch on the flowered wallpaper" (26), not as the "unfortunate boy" (23) she had begged to be allowed to see. In contrast, Grete addresses Gregor directly, "You, Gregor," which were the "first words she had addressed directly to him since his metamorphosis." The extremes of these two perspectives—"gigantic brown blotch" and "You, Gregor!"—reveal the breadth of possible interpretations of Gregor in his metamorphosed state, from inanimate blotch to human brother with whom one can speak. Grete's naming and direct address draws Gregor out of his forgetfulness and back into connection with his humanity, particularly into his role as brother. He once again desires to help Grete and to "give his sister some sort of advice, as in the old days" (27). To do so he has to "tear himself loose by force" (27) from the fur lady, in a symbolic move away from his animality and toward his humanity. Leaving behind his substitute animal mate, he rushes after Grete, his substitute human mate. But, as in his initial emergence from his room, his efforts have a shattering effect, this time on the bottles of medicine that Grete drops on seeing Gregor. Like the scattered newspapers that give visual form to the scattering of linguistic and hermeneutical efforts that takes place when Gregor first emerges from his room, so the shattered medicine bottles suggest the shattering of any hope for recovery or healing.

When Gregor's father hears Grete's account of what has just taken place—"Mother fainted, but she's better now. Gregor's broken out" (27)—he puts the "worst interpretation on Grete's all-too-brief announcement and assume[s] that Gregor [is] guilty of some outrage" (27). Gregor tries to communicate his innocence by rushing to the door of his room, since he has "neither the time nor the ability to enlighten" his father with words (27). But his father refuses to be a good reader of Gregor's actions; he is in "no mood to notice such subtleties" (27). Here we see a resurrection of the father, bearing an uncanny resemblance to that of the father in "The Judgment." Like Mr. Bendemann, Mr. Samsa used to "lie wearily buried in bed" (27), sit all day "in his bathrobe" (28), have "difficulty getting to his feet" (28), and "shuffle along with great effort" (28) using a "crutch-handled cane" (28) when the family went for a rare walk. Now, at the sight of him, Gregor thinks to himself, "He had not really imagined his father looking like this. . . . And yet, and yet—was this still his father?" (27). Like Mr. Bendemann, who reveals the ability to reclaim all the power he alleges his son has usurped, Mr. Samsa is now the one commanding respect, "holding himself very erect, dressed in a tight-fitting blue uniform with gold buttons" (28).[21] The photo of Gregor "from his army days in a lieutenant's uniform, his hand on his sword, a carefree smile on his lips, demanding respect for his bearing and his rank" (12), which hangs on the wall opposite the main door to his room, is replaced by the real presence of his father in uniform. Gregor is shocked by the "gigantic size of the soles of his boots" (28), calling to mind the moment when Georg Bendemann realizes his father is a "giant of a man."[22] Both fathers in their resurrected states resemble Kafka's father.

His father refuses to read the signs Gregor seeks to communicate with his body and instead bombards him with apples from his pockets—those secret sources of power in Kafka's fiction. His shift from newspaper and cane to apples as his weapons of choice maps onto the changes he himself has undergone in the two months since Gregor's metamorphosis. The cane and newspaper were representative objects of his life before the metamorphosis as someone who could not work, walked with difficulty, and stayed at home reading the paper.[23] After the metamorphosis, the father has undergone a resurrection of sorts: he has a job, no longer needs a cane, and wears a handsome uniform. He has become the breadwinner—or "apple winner"—of the family and likewise his weapons of attack, apples, are symbolic both of his everyday activities and of his movement from the linguistic realm of the newspaper to the physical realm of work. That the weapons with which this resurrected father overpowers his son come from his pocket echoes the connection between pockets and paternal power in Kafka's "Letter to His Father" and "The Judgment."

Wounded by an apple that lodges in his back and begins to fester, Gregor experiences a rapid physical decline. The wound, "a visible souvenir" (29) of the father's aggression against Gregor, hampers his movement, in the same way that the furniture had previously, only this time the hindrance is internal rather than external. He hardly sleeps or eats. However, the wound, though physically debilitating, brings some improvement in his relationship with his family. It reminds his father that Gregor is, in fact, his son and not an intruder to be driven from the family's midst:

> Gregor's serious wound . . . seemed to have reminded even his father that Gregor was a member of the family, in spite of his present pathetic and repulsive shape, who could not be treated as an enemy; that, on the contrary, it was the commandment of family duty to swallow their disgust and endure him, endure him, and nothing more. (29)

Though it was the voice of his mother, the linguistic realm, that reminded Gregor of his humanity, it is his wounded body, the physical realm, that reminds his father and the others of Gregor's humanity and his identity as a member of the family. However, this recognition of Gregor as a family member brings about a declining state of well-being in the family. Though his door is now often left open in the evenings, as some sort of token recognition of his membership in the family, there is little conversation going on for him to hear. The "overworked and exhausted family" (31) spends its evenings mostly in silence. Family heirlooms are sold, three boarders are taken in, presumably to help with the financial situation, and an irritableness seems to have "infected the whole family" (32), who think they have been singled out for misfortune.

The Resolution of Ambiguity through Definitive Interpretation

It is the scene with the boarders that initiates the final turning point in the family's relationship with Gregor. One evening Grete plays the violin for them. The parents anxiously watch her hands, more concerned with the impression she will make than with the music itself—an interest in her body as a means to economic and social capital that is continued at the end of the story. The boarders stand close enough to read the music and then withdraw in irritation, deeming her playing unsatisfying. Gregor is the only listener who finds it beautiful; he is "attracted by the playing" (35) and feels "as if the way to the unknown nourishment he longed for [was] coming to light" (36).[24] He imagines a life of intimacy with his sister; somehow the music suggests to him the possibility of a link to humanity other than the linguistic. Might music be a language that could unite his conflicting drives and instincts, that could reconnect him to his sister, that could provide a language in which he and his family could communicate?

However, as in the scene when his mother and sister remove furniture from his room, his desire for connection with the human realm quickly turns territorial, and he is soon imagining how he can get his sister, like the lady in the fur, into his room, keep her there, and stave off intruders with "his nightmarish looks [which] would be of use to him; he would be at all the doors of his room at the same time and hiss and spit at aggressors" (36). He fantasizes that his sister would once again be able to understand the words he says and would gratefully stay with him "of her own free will" (36), sitting beside him on the couch, listening to him, and allowing him to kiss her on her bare neck (in contrast to the fur lady's neck, which is covered by the fur boa). However, this fantasy is soon dispelled when the boarders notice him.

Oddly enough, upon seeing him, the boarders at first find him entertaining; they are "not at all upset" (36) at the sight of him. In this response, they are like the cleaning woman who earlier in the story shows no sign of disturbance at the sight of Gregor. When she encounters him, she is "not really repelled by Gregor" (33); she merely stands at the door and watches him with curiosity. Unlike the office manager, the cleaning woman and the boarders have no knowledge of Gregor's human background; he is unambiguously a bug to them. This narrative detail suggests that the disruption Gregor's metamorphosis causes his family and the manager may have less to do with physical appearances and more to do with what his metamorphosis uncovers in his relations with the office and with his family. Gregor is not a hermeneutically disruptive text to those who have no knowledge of his human background.

Although the boarders are not disturbed by Gregor's identity—in fact, one smiles to the other two at the sight of him, and Gregor's appearance seems to be "entertaining them more than the violin-playing" (36)—they do demand an explanation for his presence there. Though he is not a hermeneutically disruptive text for them, he is repulsive, covered as he is with dust and hair and bits of garbage. They do not want an explanation for his metamorphosis but for why he is in the apartment. Surely something of this sort should not be inside. Whereas the appearance of Gregor's metamorphosed body disrupted the hermeneutical activities of his parents and the office manager in the first section, his appearance near the end of the story elicits the desire for an explanation in the boarders. To them Gregor is not a hermeneutically disruptive text but rather one whose presence demands an explanation. To them, the answer is clear: that thing has no place in the household.

Yet the family has no explanation to give the boarders for Gregor's presence in their midst: "That is our son/brother-turned-monstrous-vermin" would hardly be satisfactory. The family is faced with the uninterpretable text in the context of needing to interpret it. In response to this hermeneutical frustration—the conflict between the need for and the difficulty of interpretation—the father reenacts his resurrection to power. This time it is the boarders, rather than Gregor, who are driven back to their rooms: "He completely forgot any respect still due his tenants. He drove them on and kept on driving" (37). Once again, those who have called for an interpretation are silenced.

Gregor's reemergence from his room reminds the family of their hermeneutical frustration—their inability to come up with a definitive interpretation of him because he is both a repulsive bug and their own human relative Gregor. Their patience comes to an end. Whereas his wound served earlier to remind the family that Gregor was indeed part of the family, the scene with the boarders causes them to move in the opposite direction: to forget his familial connection to them, to consider getting rid of him, and to stop thinking that he "could not be treated as an enemy" (29). Grete goes so far as to say, "I won't pronounce the name of my brother in front of this monster" (37). In this single sentence, Gregor is separated into two identities: on the one hand, he is a monster, the cause of their "constant torture" (38); on the other, he is Gregor, Grete's brother who will now be recognized in name and memory only.

Grete decides to put an end to the frustration caused by this ambiguous text, claiming that their living conditions have become unbearable. She declares that the source of all their problems lies in the fact that they have been thinking of this creature as Gregor, as a human being rather than as a monster: "You just have to try to get rid of the idea that it's Gregor. Believing it for so long, that is our real misfortune" (38). Their problem, she declares, is interpretive. They have gone about interpreting this monster in the wrong way. In fact, it is the wrong interpretation that has been their "real misfortune," which has weighed the family down even more than the bug itself.

In fact, Grete argues, "if it were Gregor, he would have realized long ago that it isn't possible for human beings to live with such a creature, and he would have gone away of his own free will. Then we wouldn't have a brother, but we'd be able to go on living and honor his memory" (38). Because this creature is still here, she argues, it is obviously not her brother. In other words, Gregor would have been able to interpret his metamorphosis correctly—as an event that rendered him unacceptable for family life—and he would have left long ago. Sokel highlights the key role of interpretation in Grete's view: "His sister accepts the metamorphosis as an empirical fact, as something which certainly could have happened to her brother. The 'miracle' of the metamorphosis itself is not put in question, but only its interpretation."[25] Thus, Grete does not call into question whether this bug before them *could* be Gregor; she fully recognizes the possibility that such a metamorphosis could happen. Rather, she insists that this is not Gregor because if he had become such a bug, he would have left them in peace. Stanley Corngold points out an important change Kafka made in the manuscript that underscores this move on Grete's part; he writes, "Kafka wrote in the MS [manuscript], 'We must try to get rid of him,' but then made this change of pronoun sealing Gregor's fate as an insect, an It, eligible for the harshest treatment."[26] The fact that "it" has remained with them for so long proves that "it" is not Gregor but a bug. She resolves the hesitation before the ambiguous text of Gregor's identity and fulfills the hermeneutical drive, the desire for complete interpretation, by declaring Gregor to be unambiguously a bug.

Grete interprets Gregor as vermin in order to be rid of him; by excluding him from the family circle, she rids them of the obligation to be patient with him and to treat him as a family member. The question,

Is this creature in our midst Gregor?, is definitively answered in the negative: it is not Gregor; it is vermin.[27] In doing so, Grete sweeps away any responsibility the family has toward Gregor, just as Gregor's body will soon be swept away by the cleaning woman. The tie that binds the family to the bug is a matter of interpretation, according to Grete, and she manages to untie it.[28] Grete resolves the conflict between the need for and the impossibility of interpreting the metamorphosis by misreading the text of Gregor's metamorphosed body.

Kafka suggests Grete's important role in the family's final turn away from Gregor when he describes her in a letter to Grete Bloch: "The heroine's name is Grete and she doesn't discredit you, at least not in the first section. Later on, though, when the agony becomes too great, she withdraws, embarks on a life of her own, and leaves the one who needs her."[29] One way to withdraw from the text that invites interpretive activity but frustrates definitive interpretation is to misread it, to interpret unambiguously the ambiguous text. If interpretation is a form of engagement, the claim to have arrived at a definitive interpretation is a form of disengagement, withdrawal, for it brings about the end of the activity of interpretation. It may also be a betrayal of those who do not fit established categories, who may need us to live with their complexity and the tension it creates in us. The family misreads Gregor in an attempt to overcome the frustration of a situation in which it seems impossible yet necessary to interpret. By misreading the text that is Gregor's metamorphosed body, they do, as Harold Bloom would describe it, "clear imaginative space for themselves."[30] However, when the text being read is a person, there is much more at stake than imaginative space. By misreading Gregor, these "strong poets" abandon their duty to "endure" him, they "leave the one who needs them" and call for his death.

"Was He an Animal?"

Gregor's reemergence from the room causes the family to abandon their interpretation of him as their family member, but it also occasions his own reconsideration of his identity. He wonders at his response to the music: "Was he an animal, that music could move him so?" (36). The wording of the text is ambiguous, forbidding the reader from knowing whether Gregor's response seems to him to make him like or unlike an animal: was he so much an animal that he was thus moved by the music? or, how could he be an animal if music could move him in such a manner? But the fact that the question is raised in Gregor's mind is key. Up until this point, Gregor has not been reflective about his changed identity. Whereas the family's reconsideration of his identity is elicited by their humiliation in front of the boarders—that is, in the social realm—Gregor's is elicited by his response to the music, in the aesthetic realm.

Grete moves through the questions surrounding Gregor's identity with swift blows—he is not Gregor, he is not human, he is a monster—making a complete turnaround from the family's earlier stance of treating Gregor as a family member, albeit a repulsive one.[31] As if submitting to her proclamation, Gregor takes up Grete's terms for human existence—that if he were really Gregor, really human, he would have left by now—and makes them his own, accepting Grete's division of him into a monstrous body to be disposed of and a human identity to be remembered by name alone. Gregor relinquishes his paradoxical identity and submits to his sister's judgment. He decides that he must die: "His conviction that he would have to disappear was, if possible, even firmer than his sister's" (39). The price for resolving the hermeneutical paradox that his identity constitutes is his very existence—to be human, he must die—a price that his sister is only too happy to have him pay and that Gregor, out of love for his family, is willing to pay.

Grete's definitive interpretation through misreading reveals the violence involved in resolving the ambiguity of such a text; it involves ignoring, repressing, or destroying whatever does not fit the definitive interpretation. It allows no uninterpreted remainder; it asserts complete interpretation. Gregor's acceptance of his sister's definitive interpretation results in the dissolution of his capacity to interpret and his very existence and thus reveals the violence that is done to the person who cannot or does not resist such interpretive strategies. In this situation, both the fulfillment and the dissolution of the hermeneutical drive destroy the text that Gregor's metamorphosed being constitutes—one by murderous order, the other by a suicidal obedience to it.

The ironic twist in the story is that in dying, in carrying out the death sentence that his identity as bug has prompted, Gregor fulfills the requirements for human identity that Grete has articulated: "If it were Gregor . . . he would have gone away of his own free will." Sokel highlights Gregor's submission to Grete's judgment: "Gregor carries out the death sentence on himself that his sister, as the representative of the family and of life, had pronounced on him."[32] In doing so, he reasserts his humanity. In contradiction to Rolleston, who argues that "Gregor's unwavering attachment to his own view of himself gains him a dignity untouched by death in disgusting circumstances,"[33] I contend that Gregor has been unable, throughout the story, to interpret himself, has been unable to formulate a view of himself, especially not one to which he is unwaveringly attached. It is only in his decision to die that Gregor clings to a view of himself that does not waver between his human and vermin identities. In realizing that his family cannot live with him and in moving toward death, Gregor aligns himself with humanity. In deciding to die, Gregor declares himself human. As David Eggenschwiler points out, "Gregor dies here not as a monstrous vermin (do bugs have nostrils through which a dying breath passes?) . . . but as a human being with affection, acceptance, and peace."[34]

In aligning himself with the will of the family, Gregor refutes Grete's interpretation of him as a monster and not her brother. In dying, Gregor marks his re-metamorphosis into a full human. He does what is necessary to reenter the human race: he gets rid of his verminous self. But the cost of this reentrance into humanity and into the family is death, for his verminous self is not extractable from his human self. As he dies, Gregor thinks of "his family with deep emotion and love" (39), just as Georg did when he let himself drop from the bridge. Both protagonists submit to the death sentence ordered by their family member, yet each in doing so regains his previous identity (innocent child in Georg's case, human being in Gregor's), expresses his love for his family, and refutes the very "crime" for which he has been sentenced: being a devilish human being, in Georg's case, and being not human, in Gregor's. Solely by dying and living on only in memory and in name can Gregor maintain his humanity and "remain" in the family.

"Cleansing" the Family of "Disorder"

At the end of both "The Judgment" and "The Metamorphosis," it is a cleaning person who is the last person to see the protagonist: Georg runs into the maid as he rushes down the stairs to his death; Gregor is disposed of by the cleaning woman. This connection of the removal of dirt and disorder with the death of the hermeneutically disruptive protagonist illuminates Kafka's seemingly conflicting comments on the deaths of his protagonists. In a letter to Felice about Gregor, he writes, "Cry, dearest, cry, the time for crying has come! The hero of my story died a little while ago."[35] Though the death of the protagonist is a sad event, Kafka also describes it as bringing about Gregor's reconciliation with the family when he writes to Felice: "To comfort you, I want you to know that he died peacefully enough and reconciled to all."[36] Gregor's death is paradoxically redemptive in that it psychologically and symbolically reintegrates him into the family, "reconciled to all," even as it removes him physically. The appearance of the cleaning woman symbolizes the cleansing of the family unit that costs the protagonist his life and the family one of its members.

But what sort of world is this where one has to die in order to be recognized as human, where a family member is declared not human so that he can be disposed of, where to be part of the family one has to kill himself or allow himself to die? The subversive aspect of Gregor's death is that it disproves Grete's judgment of him as not Gregor. His death is both the punishment for not being human and the proof that he is human, revealing the destructive nature of a definitive interpretation and of submitting to the terms of such an interpretation. For definitive interpretation involves misreading the ambiguity that causes hermeneutical hesitation, a hesitation that resists the temptation to erase ambiguity and simplify complexity. In Gregor's case, the hesitation is caused by his ambiguous identity. Grete definitively interprets him as bug in order to be rid of him. However, paradoxically, what Grete has erased in her interpretation, Gregor's humanity, is the very thing that most exerts itself in his death.

The way Gregor's family responds to his death supports the idea that they have divided Gregor into two manageable texts: the bug that can be disposed of and the family member they can remember. For, after his death, the family engages in rituals of mourning—not the usual response to the death of a large bug in one's home. Grete reverts to using "he" rather than "it" to refer to Gregor after his death, even though she had used "it" when pronouncing his death sentence. They all make the sign of the cross upon seeing his dead body, indicative of his status as human rather than animal.[37] The sadness of the family, evidenced by the fact that they "looked as if they had been crying" (40–41), marks Gregor's death as not merely the death of a bug or the good riddance of a burden but the loss of a family member. Further, the family takes the day off work as if a relative has died, as if they need to process and mourn his death. In his death, Gregor becomes unambiguously human to them as well.

The cheerful, lightheartedness of the cleaning woman serves as a stark contrast to the weighted emotions of the family. The woman can call his body "the stuff" (42) only because she has known him only as "that old dung beetle" (33) and not as a human being. The family's resistance to, and obvious discomfort with, the cleaning woman's attempt to tell them about how she disposed of Gregor's body highlights their unease with the false division they have made between the verminous body and their memory of Gregor: Grete and her mother lean over "as if to continue writing" (42) their letters in order to avoid looking at her. Her mention of "the stuff next door" (42) has "ruined their barely regained peace of mind" (42). The father dismisses the cleaning woman's attempt to tell her story with a "firmly outstretched hand" (42).

The father hastens her departure for the day and prevents her from describing the disposal of Gregor's body. Further, he announces that they will fire her that very night. The father's announcement reassures the women that all evidence of their deceased family member's verminous body, including its disposer, will be erased and that they will be able to live without any trace of it. This is further underscored by their subsequent decision to move out of their present apartment, chosen and lived in by Gregor, and into a smaller but better-situated one—one that has no trace or memories of Gregor's presence in their family. Thus they continue their practice of ridding themselves of all that causes them discomfort so that they can live untroubled by their history of misreading and their guilt in Gregor's death.

Now that they are rid of Gregor and will soon be rid of any trace of his existence, the Samsa family begins to focus on the future, and the pattern by which they have overcome disaster in the past reveals itself again: the parents look to their daughter as their source of hope. Given the nature of Gregor's life after the family business disaster occurred, one can only wonder what Grete's life will be like following this familial disaster. Concerning Grete's shift in status, Sokel argues that "by the self-elimination of her brother as a human being, Grete rises to monopolistic eminence and privilege in her family."[38] But this preeminence also marks her out for the parasitic plans of the parents. Previously they had lived off Gregor's wages, placed the burden of the family debt on him, hid the fact that they had money stashed away, all the while recognizing that this chained him to his job and furthered his social isolation. Now they turn to Grete with eyes large in expectation: "It occurred almost simultaneously to Mr. and Mrs. Samsa . . . that, in spite of all the troubles which had turned her cheeks pale, she had blossomed into a good-looking, shapely girl. . . . It would soon be time, too, to find her a good husband" (42). They look to her body and its capacity to attract a husband, rather than to Gregor's capacity to work and gain them money as in the past. Maurice Blanchot highlights not the horror of the parents' parasitic plans but of Grete's gesture of standing up and stretching at the end of the story. He argues that "the young sister's gesture, her movement of awakening to life, the call to the sensual on which the story ends, is the height of horror; there is nothing more frightening in the entire story."[39] The family mourns the person they have driven to death and think they have thereby disposed of their guilt. Their immediate hope in the future, with only the briefest period of mourning, suggests that they have expulsed any sense of guilt from their midst. Their definitive interpretation of the hermeneutically complex text, their deliberate misreading of its ambiguity and complexity, has enabled them to forget the violent consequences of their own interpretive practices.

The Fantastic Metamorphosis? The Hesitation between the Uncanny and the Marvelous

In depicting the violence associated with dividing Gregor's complex identity into two separate and thereby manageable identities, Kafka suggests the importance of interpreting in a way that avoids simplifying and reducing those complex identities and texts that defy our categories. At the level of genre, "The Metamorphosis," like Gregor himself, resists reduction into a clear genre. Tzvetan Todorov suggests that Kafka's works constitute a new genre, the "generalized fantastic." His discussion of the hesitation that is the crucial characteristic of the fantastic provides an illustrative way to think about the Samsa family's stance before Gregor. But it also helps us to think more about the reader's stance before the story. Further, Todorov's own activity of interpretation, like Freud's in chapter 2, offers us an example of the struggles and temptations that even the best interpreters face and to which they sometimes succumb.

Todorov argues that the fantastic is that which replicates and sustains a state of hesitation before an ambiguous event; a fantastic event is one in which the reader cannot decide whether it is a real or supernatural event. Todorov suggests that "by the hesitation it engenders, the fantastic questions precisely the existence of an irreducible opposition between the real and the unreal."[40] This parallels the fact that Gregor's transformation itself questions precisely the existence of an irreducible opposition between the human and the nonhuman, with the former mapping onto the real and the latter onto the unreal. By looking at Todorov's discussion of the fantastic and the hesitation it engenders—a hesitation that must be sustained for the fantastic to persist—the reader of Kafka's story is given insight into the way in which hesitation, or the refusal to simplify and reduce what is more complex than our interpretive categories, must also persist in order to resist hermeneutical tyranny, like Grete's judgment of Gregor.

Todorov describes the fantastic as existing on the frontier between the uncanny and the marvelous:

> The fantastic, we have seen, lasts only as long as a certain hesitation: a hesitation common to reader and character, who must decide whether or not what they perceive derives from "reality" as it exists in the common opinion. At the story's end, the reader makes a decision even if the character does not; he opts for one solution or the other, and thereby emerges from the fantastic. If he decides that the laws of reality remain intact and permit an explanation of the phenomena described, we say that the work belongs to another genre: the uncanny. If, on the contrary, he decides that new laws of nature must be entertained to account for the phenomena, we enter into the genre of the marvelous. (41)

Thus, the fantastic involves a strange event that cannot yet be interpreted as real or unreal; as soon as it is interpreted as such, it ceases to be fantastic and becomes either uncanny or marvelous. The hesitation that constitutes the fantastic is a hesitation before two opposing interpretations: "The reader . . . must decide if a certain event or phenomenon belongs to reality or to imagination, that is, must determine whether or not it is real" (167). If the reader decides the event, however strange it may be, can be explained by the rules of this world, then, says Todorov, the event is uncanny. If the event cannot be explained by the rules of this world and, hence, takes place in a wholly different world, it is marvelous. But as long as the reader hesitates between the two options and cannot categorize the event as either real or unreal, it remains fantastic.

Of course, the question of what is real and what is unreal is problematic in fiction, where everything is, in one sense, unreal. Fiction is made up. How, then, can one speak of "real" and "unreal"? What Todorov is getting at here is the interpretive framework the reader brings to the story. We read a fairy tale with a different set of interpretive tools, expectations, and concessions than we do a mystery. Though odd things happen in each, we know that at the end of the mystery, things will be explained and will appear through this explanation as events that could have happened in the world in which we live. At the end of the fairy tale, we do not expect such an explanation: though the events of a fairy tale may take place according to the rules of a world quite unlike our own and may receive some sort of explanation at the end, it will be an explanation that bears on the meaning of those events rather than on the possibility of their occurrence in our world. We do not expect to correlate the events of a fairy tale to the rules of our world.

In contrast, when confronted with the fantastic event, we cannot decide which interpretive framework to use to make sense of it. We are unable to place it in either of two possible categories, in either the uncanny (real) or the marvelous (unreal). It disrupts our categories by both fitting neither and yet having points of connection with each. In fact, the fantastic is maintained and constituted by this hesitation before the two options that are inadequate but relevant to the phenomenon. However, Todorov suggests repeatedly that the reader must or does decide one way or the other after reading a story, either that the events in it are real and belong to the world of the uncanny or that they are unreal and belong to the world of the marvelous. Hence, the fantastic describes one stage in the reading of uncanny or marvelous texts—a stage of hesitation that is resolved by choosing one interpretive frame over another.

What I have been arguing in this chapter, however, is that Kafka's story suggests that there are situations in which this decision, this resolution of hesitation, is morally culpable, does violence to the text, and erases complexity in order to arrive at a definitive interpretation. As we shall see, this is what Todorov's proposed reader of the fantastic does and what is evidenced in his own reading of the story.

The choice that Todorov poses between the uncanny and the marvelous is, at one level, also the choice between interpretability and noninterpretability; the hesitation before the choice is a hermeneutical hesitation. Can the strange event be interpreted according to the rules of our world? Or does it belong to an imaginary world in which such things happen as a matter of course and, therefore, it does not need to be interpreted and explained? The uncanny, the marvelous, and the fantastic all disrupt the hermeneutical drive of the reader, and each is defined, in part, by this disruption. The uncanny is that which finally submits to or fulfills the drive, with the conclusion that the events are interpretable, however strange; the marvelous is that which finally dissolves the drive, because in an imaginary world, a strange event does not need to be interpreted or explained; and the fantastic is that which sustains the drive yet leaves it unfulfilled. According to Todorov, the fantastic is temporary; it exists only until the reader has chosen her interpretive pathway: the uncanny or the marvelous.

At the end of his book, Todorov describes Kafka's texts as constituting a generalized fantastic. By this he means that traditionally the fantastic event occurs in a seemingly normal world, but in the generalized fantastic the event has been expanded to a whole world: "What in the first world was an exception here becomes the rule" (174). In the generalized fantastic, the protagonist no longer partakes of the hesitation before the fantastic event; he has become part of the fantastic world and is himself fantastic. The hesitation that is usually (though not always) shared by the protagonist and the reader in the face of the fantastic event becomes, in the generalized fantastic, the reader's unshared hesitation in the face of a strange world. Protagonist and reader no longer read the strange events of the story in the same way. It is the hermeneutical drive of the reader alone that is sustained yet unfulfilled in this hesitation.

Todorov undercuts his insights by stating that the world of Kafka's fiction is "entirely bizarre, as abnormal as the very event to which it affords a background" and "no longer has anything to do with the real" (173). It is precisely because the reader of Kafka's fiction *cannot* deem it to be *entirely* bizarre, *cannot* interpret it as real or unreal, and *cannot* confidently state that it has *nothing* to do with the real, but rather can only stand in hesitation between these two options, that it remains fantastic. If the reader could say that it was unreal or entirely bizarre, then Kafka's fiction would be located, according to Todorov's own scheme, in the realm of the marvelous, the unreal. Likewise, by calling the world of Kafka's fiction entirely bizarre, he contradicts his own description of the story as increasingly natural: "'The Metamorphosis' starts from a supernatural event, and during the course of the narrative gives it an increasingly *natural* atmosphere" (171; emphasis mine).[41] How can the story be both entirely bizarre and increasingly natural?

To say that a work is fantastic is to say that one is unable to interpret it as realistic or unrealistic, as natural or bizarre; it is to say that both options are open but neither can be chosen, that both are necessary as options but neither is attainable as a choice. Thus if Todorov is right about the world of Kafka's fiction having nothing to do with the real, or if he is right about the world of Kafka's story becoming natural, he is wrong about Kafka's works being fantastic.

And contrary to Todorov's claim concerning the chronology of the reader's hesitation in the traditional fantastic—that "its function has been to *prepare* the way for the perception of the unheard-of event" (171; emphasis mine)—the hesitation that constitutes the fantastic is, according to Todorov himself, a *response to*, rather than a *preparation for*, the unheard-of event:

> An event—an action—occurs which proceeds from the supernatural (or from the pseudo-supernatural); this action then provokes a reaction in the implicit reader (and generally in the hero of the story). It is this *reaction* which we describe as "hesitation," and the texts which generate it, as fantastic. (103; emphasis mine)

In the same section, Todorov goes so far as to equate the fantastic with the reaction of hesitation: "The text may emphasize *the fantastic (i.e., the reaction)*" (103; emphasis mine). Nowhere but in his discussion of Kafka's works does Todorov speak of the hesitation as a preparatory experience, and when he speaks of it in that context, it is only to claim that since this preparatory hesitation is not present in "The Metamorphosis," it cannot be considered as belonging to the traditional fantastic.

If this hesitation were in fact preparatory, what would it be a hesitation about? Previously, Todorov has defined the hesitation as being about deciding whether the event is real or unreal. If the event has not yet happened when the hesitation occurs, it certainly cannot be a hesitation about whether the event is real or unreal. Therefore, either the hesitation that constitutes the fantastic is a response to the event and is lacking in Kafka's story, thereby pointing to its divergence from the traditional fantastic, or this hesitation is present in the story and therefore points to a similarity between the genre of the fantastic and "The Metamorphosis." Because the hesitation constitutive of the fantastic is a *response* to the fantastic event rather than a *preparation* for it, Todorov cannot argue that because there is no hesitation preparing the way for Gregor's metamorphosis (since it is reported in the first sentence of the story), the story diverges from the fantastic.

Todorov's arguments for why "The Metamorphosis" belongs neither to the traditional fantastic nor to the marvelous are somewhat weak. Todorov argues that it cannot be marvelous because "the marvelous implies that we are plunged into a world whose laws are totally different from what they are in our own and in consequence that the supernatural events which occur are in no way disturbing" (171–72). However, two pages later, he argues that "in Kafka, the supernatural event no longer provokes hesitation, for the world described is entirely bizarre, as abnormal as the very event to which it affords a background" (173). The distinction between a world whose laws are totally different from ours and a world that is entirely bizarre is not made clear. And yet it is the difference between these two that somehow for Todorov marks the difference between the marvelous and Kafka's story.

Kafka's writing constitutes a generalized fantastic and sustains a generalized hermeneutical hesitation in the reader. As opposed to the marvelous, the fantastic calls for interpretation; as opposed to the uncanny, the fantastic effectively resists definitive interpretation. In Kafka's works, the hesitation of the generalized fantastic becomes generalized in two ways: first, in becoming a response to the whole world of the text, rather than just one event; and second (a corollary of the first), in becoming a hesitation both about the real and the unreal and more broadly about the means to make such a decision—that is, the activity of interpretation itself.

An interesting parallel can be seen between the hesitation before the genre options of the uncanny and the marvelous and the hesitation before the identity options of "monster" and "human." According to Todorov the interpreter chooses one and thereby ends his hesitation and dissolves the fantastic; so also Grete ends her hesitation, and that of her parents, and brings about the dissolution of Gregor by declaring him a monster, by choosing one option for Gregor's identity. Like the hesitation between the real and the unreal in Todorov's fantastic, the hesitation before interpretation in the Kafkan text cannot be resolved without dissolving something. Usually it is the protagonist himself who undergoes this dissolution because one of the other characters refuses to remain in the state of hesitation and instead decides to resolve that hesitation once and for all. Grete refuses to live with Gregor's ambiguous identity and decides to resolve the hesitation by redefining Gregor as a monster and thereby getting rid of him.

Like Grete, the reader is faced with a text that troubles his existing categories. "The Metamorphosis" places the reader in an unresolvable state of hermeneutical hesitation, hesitation before the choice of whether to interpret Kafka's world as real or unreal and hesitation before interpretation itself.

"The Metamorphosis" represents the temptations inherent in interpreting that which does not fit the categories we have to make sense of things. Gregor's metamorphosis into a new kind of being, one that cannot be declared human or not human without reductively erasing some part of his new identity, constitutes a challenge to those who engage in interpretation as one might solve a puzzle, arriving at the answer and sighing with satisfaction at its completion. Both Gregor himself and Kafka's story about him present a challenge to their "readers" and offer the opportunity to learn a different way of engaging with otherness—a way that seeks to understand, that draws near, that avoids erasure even when forgetting some aspects that might make the task of interpretation much easier. The reader may be able to dispose of the text as the cleaning lady disposes of Gregor's body and then look to the future with "The Metamorphosis" clearly behind him, just as the family looks to the future with Gregor's metamorphosis clearly behind them, but if we have read carefully and closely, we will realize the violence of such an act.

The Samsa family misreads Gregor in order to be rid of him; Gregor accepts this misreading of his identity and abandons his own efforts to preserve his complex identity. The reader, however, is aware that Gregor is still both a bug and a human being, that there are two seemingly incompatible interpretations of him, and that it is impossible to make a choice between them without misinterpreting Gregor's identity. For the reader, remaining in the hermeneutical hesitation before the two options is the only viable choice. In depicting the (horrific) results of both Grete's totalizing definition and misreading of Gregor and Gregor's subservient submission to that reading, Kafka points to the need for interpretive practices that do not erase, claim completion, or destroy.

What does this hermeneutical drama tell the reader of "The Metamorphosis"? The difficulty in interpreting the story is obvious, but so are the dangers of not engaging in the act of interpretation. As Charles Bernheimer suggests, "Kafka's texts offer their readers a powerful dramatization of the life-and-death issues at stake in the act of reading."[42] Because of their multivalence, to claim to interpret Kafka's texts definitively, by forgetting aspects of the text that disrupt that interpretation, not only constitutes bad reading but also does violence to the text by erasing those aspects of it that do fit neatly within our categories. This is the temptation to which the family has succumbed at the end of the story. To withdraw from the activity of interpretation, either in despair or subservience, leads to the end of the reader as reader. This is the fate that befalls Gregor; unwilling or unable to interpret himself, he falls prey to the interpretive strategies of his family. Kafka's text points out the necessity of engaging in interpretive activity as an ongoing process, forgoing the temptation and violence of definitive interpretation but also resisting it through active engagement in the interpretive process.

The Kafkan text calls for interpretive activity and resists definitive interpretation by its reader. The text's resistance does not make it a playful tease nor a stubborn child resisting interpretation nor a potential victim defending itself against the ravages of the interpreter. The Kafkan text itself teaches us about interpretation as engagement in the effort to understand, accompanied by a hesitation that acknowledges its own limitations (it can never arrive at a complete interpretation) and its temptations—it must resist its own desire for mastery.

Although hesitation has the negative connotation of indecisiveness and a lack of confidence, we might rethink hesitation as the ability to withstand the temptation to simplify what is complex, reduce what unsettles us by its plurality, or claim completion where such is but a fantasy. In this sense, hesitation is a stronger, more difficult task. It is also a more creative one, since it keeps the relationship of engagement and the process of interpretation in play. Kafka described himself as a "hesitation before birth,"[43] and we might rethink what that means as being not related to a stillbirth but rather something more akin to Hannah Arendt's understanding of natality, of the always present possibility for something new to arise, for something to be created that was not there before, of the human capacity to invent and to imagine things and the world and the person standing before you otherwise.

Kafka's text also suggests the need for creatively responding to new phenomena, new identities, by allowing for the creation of new categories and genres. And yet the cost of this openness is high. Kafka himself describes it as "agony"—this is not the joyful depiction of creative possibilities but the call to a sometimes ethical stance of resisting closure, comfort, and completion. He offers us a challenge for how we think about the contours of humanity, how we define the human, and whom or what we seek to exclude in claiming that something or someone is not human.

Chapter 4

✦

The Ethics of Attention and the Meaning of Pain

Kafka's "In the Penal Colony" and Levinas's "Useless Suffering"

The first three chapters have highlighted the hermeneutical tyranny of the father or family; this chapter moves beyond the private walls of the home to a penal colony, from interpersonal authority to political and societal authority. Instead of facing the tyrannical father or family, the impotent subject faces a whole penal system in Kafka's story "In the Penal Colony." This chapter looks at the connections between interpretation, power, and violence with a focus not merely on the power to interpret the other, refute his interpretations, and make him submit to one's interpretation of him but also, even further, on the power to control his very interpretive faculty. In short, it looks at tyrannical efforts to script the other's interpretations, as well as his very mode and means of interpretation. The impotent subject here reads and interprets in the manner prescribed by the tyranny and produces those interpretations scripted by it. This is a more insidious form of hermeneutical tyranny, one that may or may not end in the subject's death but which takes over his agency so completely that it is not that he is left with no voice, but no self.

An interesting shift in perspective takes place in Kafka's "In the Penal Colony": rather than focusing on the interaction between father and son or tyrant and his subject, Kafka adds a new character into the drama of hermeneutical tyranny—the witness to or reader of that drama. Whereas "The Metamorphosis" added other family members to the drama and included small roles for third-party characters like the office manager and the boarders, in Kafka's "In the Penal Colony," one of the two major characters is initially a third party, merely an observer, to the tyranny, and the impotent subject, the condemned man, plays only a minor role.

The explorer visiting the colony moves through a series of shifting third-party roles: uninterested guest, observer, bystander, witness, advocate, and accomplice—roles that correlate to shifting levels of involvement, responsibility, and guilt. The explorer is particularly of interest in a study of interpretation in Kafka's work since he is arguably the character most aligned with the reader in all of Kafka's corpus. That he might serve as a model (or countermodel) for Kafka's reader is worth considering as we explore Kafka's interpretation of interpretation. How the explorer reads in the penal colony has important implications for how the reader reads "In the Penal Colony."

To begin an exploration of the hermeneutical tyranny operative in Kafka's "In the Penal Colony," I focus on the characters' shifts of attention that take place in the first part of the story—for example, from distraction to attention, from indifference to admiration. The story's own relentless focus on these shifts draws our attention to them and highlights their importance. Then I look at the theatrical and scripted nature of the judicial and penal processes in the colony, drawing on the work of Michel Foucault. Finally, I explore the ethical implications of those shifts of attention and the scripted punishment by reading Emmanuel Levinas's essay "Useless Suffering" in tandem with Kafka's story. The penal colony officer's description of the prisoner's experience in the execution apparatus can be read as a counternarrative to Levinas's phenomenology of suffering. In both texts, the kind and measure of attention paid to suffering is crucial.

This paired reading of Kafka and Levinas does two important things: First, it sheds light on Levinas's phenomenology of suffering, which is itself difficult to understand. Second, it helps us to see the invisibility or irrelevance of pain *as suffering* in Kafka's story: the officer and the explorer acknowledge that pain is part of the process of the apparatus—thus the pain is visible to both—but neither registers any empathy, concern, or outrage about the fact that the machine tortures the condemned man for twelve hours, thus pain *as suffering* is invisible or irrelevant to them. The pain the machine inflicts is made visible and visceral to the reader by the detailed description of it offered by the officer.

Some readers, however, seem to ignore the visceral details of suffering depicted in the story and have themselves seemed to follow the reading practices of the officer and explorer in seeing the machine not as a torture apparatus but as a machine of meaning making;[1] they read the machine metaphorically and so avoid the messy details of vomit and blood and spit. Stanley Corngold has criticized these overly abstract readings of "In the Penal Colony" and their erasure of its physicality: "There is a good deal of difference between how the story has come down to us, as a systematically pure and grave conceptual meditation, on the one hand; and, on the other, how it actually reads."[2] How might we read and interpret the story differently if we first learn about reading and interpretation from the story itself? Rather than replicate the characters' inattention to suffering, we might follow the textual cues to pay attention to it and learn from the disastrous results of their inattention. The story offers a graphic illustration of the ways in which the infliction of pain is justified by individuals and institutions like governments, who refuse to respond to or even recognize the suffering they cause. In short, Levinas's urging about the crucial role that attention to the suffering of the other should play in our efforts to live together, build a just society, and prevent or lessen tyranny of all sorts, on the one hand, and his condemnation of the ways in which suffering is instead often justified and used, on the other, may surprisingly find support in Kafka's story.

Shifting Attention

"In the Penal Colony" opens with the officer explaining the process of execution to the visiting explorer just before the process is about to begin. The officer is the public representative of this penal system; indeed, it seems he may be its only representative, given the fact that the former commandant of the colony who designed it is dead and the rest of the colony, including the new commandant, seems either uninterested or hostile to the penal process. As the officer's explanation progresses, it becomes clear that he wants the explorer to become its advocate before the new commandant. But this can happen only if the officer is able to ensure that the explorer interprets the workings of the machine correctly. There are a number of challenges to this task: first, the process is not self-evident and requires the officer to explain it ahead of time to the explorer; second, the explorer is initially completely uninterested; and third, when his interest does begin to dawn, it is at first directed toward the officer himself rather than the execution machine, and then toward the judicial process rather than the process of punishment the officer is trying to explain.

The four "onstage" characters in Kafka's "In the Penal Colony" engage in a kind of dance, moving between indifference and fascination, distraction and attention. They move between these poles of engagement, surprising us by what they pay attention to and even more by what they ignore. We are told of the explorer's indifference only to be told a few paragraphs later of his growing interest. The officer's fascination with the machine is paired with his inattention to the explorer's indifference to what the officer is saying. This movement between the poles of indifference and fascination is important precisely because the narrative voice of the story pays so much attention to it. Each sentence seems to bring some new report about a shift in, or continuation of, someone's level of engagement with something or someone around him, suggesting that we the readers ought to pay attention to who is paying attention . . . and to what. In short, the story's own focus on attention draws our attention as readers. And, as we shall see when we turn to Levinas's essay, the focus of our attention—what we pay attention to and how we do so—has important ethical implications. In fact, it becomes evident that paying attention is itself an ethical activity of utmost importance.

From the first sentence of the story, we learn of the officer's focus on and high regard for the machine used to execute prisoners in the colony: he calls it a "remarkable piece of apparatus" and views it with "a certain air of admiration."[3] He actively attends to the machine, creeping beneath it and climbing up a ladder to make adjustments. Tasks below his stature as an officer—ones a mechanic might be expected to do—he performs with "great zeal" (140). He is distracted from his work only by his own mention of the former commandant, who used to rule the colony and designed the machine. With pride the officer recounts his own participation in the machine's development and completion, though he adds admiringly that "the credit for inventing it belongs to [the former commandant] alone" (141).

In contrast, the visiting explorer to whom he is talking shows no interest in the machine and pays little attention to what the officer is saying. Like the rest of the colony, which seems to ignore the morning's event, he does not "betray much interest in this execution" (140) and seems to be there only out of politeness, having been invited by the current commandant of the colony. These narrative details might be read as covering up a hidden interest—after all, the words "betray" and "seem" suggest that the perspective from which these details are given can register only the outward appearance of the explorer and not his inner feelings—but the next paragraph tells us that what seems to be the case is indeed so: "The explorer did not much care about the apparatus and walked up and down behind the prisoner with almost visible indifference" (140).[4]

The other two figures present—the condemned man and the soldier guarding him—provide a mirror image of the officer and the explorer in terms of their attentiveness. Like the officer, the condemned man is focused, though on the officer's explanation rather than the machine itself. He is a "stupid-looking, wide-mouthed creature with bewildered hair and face" (140)—hardly the image of the officer in his elaborate uniform working with seeming expertise—yet the condemned man reveals a surprising capacity for attentiveness, which is particularly striking given that the crime for which he is being executed began with his inattention, his falling asleep at his post. The fact that the officer is speaking in French (a language unknown to the prisoner) makes it "all the more remarkable, therefore, that the prisoner [is] nonetheless making an effort to follow the officer's explanations" (142). Likewise, the soldier, in his lack of attention, mirrors the explorer; in fact, we are told explicitly that he seems to be "in much the same condition as the explorer" (142). He is indifferent to all that is going on and is "paying no attention to anything" (142). He leans against his rifle, his head hangs down, and he falls asleep—hardly the stance of a soldier guarding a prisoner about to be executed, and particularly surprising given the fact that the condemned man's infractions began with his falling asleep at his post.

The story begins with this theatrical scene of four characters, with an execution machine in their midst, in which the economy of attention keeps shifting. Initially their interactions are characterized by a displacement of either attention or understanding: The officer speaks to the explorer, but the explorer is uninterested and barely listening; the officer, for his part, hardly notices that the explorer is not listening, so intent is he on the adjustments he is making while he is talking. The prisoner listens attentively to the officer but cannot understand him since the officer speaks in French. The soldier, who is supposed to be paying attention to the prisoner in his role as guard, falls asleep. This almost farcical displacement of attention raises questions about the possibilities of reading, interpretation, and understanding among these characters, even as the officer moves on to offer an incredible story about these very activities under even more unlikely circumstances.

The explorer's initial indifference toward the officer's explanation of the machine is interrupted by his interest in the officer's uniform. He remarks on the weight of the uniform's fabric, saying, "These uniforms are too heavy for the tropics, surely" (140). And though he glances briefly—"for a fleeting moment" (141)—into the pit, beside which he has been made to sit, it is again the officer's uniform that most catches his attention. We are told:

> All the more did he admire the officer, who in spite of his tight-fitting full-dress uniform coat, amply befrogged and weighed down by epaulettes, was pursuing his subject with such enthusiasm and, besides talking, was still tightening a screw here and there with a spanner. (142)

The explorer's admiration for the officer is already in the process of increasing ("all the more did he admire the officer") by the time the reader learns of it; this admiration, which seems to come from nowhere, mirrors the officer's admiration for the machine. However, the explorer's admiration is focused not on what the officer is saying, for we are told that the explorer has "not been listening very attentively" (142), but on the enthusiasm with which the officer is saying it and the fact that he is doing so despite the heat and his heavy uniform. Note that the description of the workings of a torture machine are referred to merely as "his subject," as if the explorer has not yet even noticed what the officer is talking about, while the description of the officer's uniform is weighed down with details, even as the uniform itself is "weighed down by epaulettes."

Thus, the explorer is interested in the aesthetics of the officer's performance, its form rather than its content: the costume he wears and the enthusiasm with which he delivers his lines. As becomes apparent, the officer's admiration for the machine and his view of justice are also largely aesthetic, focused on the spectacle of justice and the performance of interpretation rather than on their actual occurrence or the content of what is interpreted.

The explorer underscores his inattention to the content of what the officer is saying when he interrupts the officer with a few short questions that either repeat words the officer has just spoken or request information he has already given. For example, as the officer explains, the bed "is completely covered with a layer of cotton wool; you'll find out why later. On this cotton wool . . ." (142); a few moments later, when the officer has gone on to explain the straps and the felt gag that is put into the prisoner's mouth, the explorer asks, "Is that cotton wool?" (143). The lapse in time between the officer's mention of the wool and the explorer's question about it, as well as the fact that the officer has already answered the question the explorer asks, highlights the fact that the explorer has not been listening to what the officer is saying.

A strange thread ties together the few elements that initially draw the explorer's attention: they have to do with fabric—not the sort of thing one thinks of as of particular interest in the context of an execution machine and thus underscoring the aesthetic sense of his budding interest.[5] The officer mentions the harrow; the explorer asks, "The Harrow?" (142). The German word translated "harrow," *die Egge*, has two meanings: an agricultural machine and selvage,[6] or "the edge of a fabric that is woven so that it will not fray or ravel" or "an ornamental fringe at either end of an oriental rug."[7] When the explorer asks, "Die Egge?," the officer states that "die Egge" is a good name for the middle part of the machine because it "works something like a harrow," though "with much more artistic skill" (142), suggesting the first meaning of *die Egge*—that is, the agricultural machine, but with an added aesthetic component. However, the second meaning echoes the explorer's focus on aesthetic elements, both the ornamentation of the officer's uniform, along with the "two fine ladies' handkerchiefs under the collar of his uniform" (140), and the exotic nature of foreign fabric. While the officer is trying to ensure that the explorer will correctly interpret the workings of the machine, the explorer is focused on aesthetic details that are completely unrelated to the execution. The explorer's aesthetic engagement is at odds with the interpretational task the officer wants him to perform.

The explorer's interest in the officer's uniform, the harrow, and the cotton wool and his seeming indifference to what the officer is actually saying suggest the explorer's lack of interest in understanding the penal apparatus. We have been told he accepted the invitation to witness the execution only out of politeness, not because he had any interest in it. However, his focus of attention is still rather odd given the circumstances: he comments on the heat and the officer's uniform rather than on the death that is about to take place; he looks at the cotton wool before he has even glanced at the machine itself. That he sees merely the surface of things and observes minor details reveals his detachment and disengagement with the larger issues at hand. The explorer's initial lack of attention to the execution machine contrasts sharply with the officer's obsessive fascination with it.

But soon this limited interest shifts as the explorer's wandering gaze leads to more than cursory observation. The officer takes the explorer's hand and runs it over the cotton wool, almost as a street vendor might draw the hand of a casual browser over a fine silk to arouse his desire to buy. However, the desire the officer seeks to arouse is the desire to understand the "remarkable piece of apparatus" (140). As he guides the explorer's hand over the cotton wool, the officer explains that it is "specially prepared"; adds tantalizingly, "I'll tell you presently what it's for" (143); and then grows quiet. The browsing observer's attention has been caught: "The explorer already felt a dawning interest in the apparatus" (143). So much so that whereas before he had felt that "the glare of the sun in the shadeless valley was altogether too strong" (142), making listening to the officer's explanation of the machine and collecting one's thoughts "difficult" (142), now, after touching the cotton wool, he "shelter[s] his eyes from the sun with one hand" (143) so that he can look at the machine. He notices that it is a "huge affair" (143).[8]

At this point, a shift in attention occurs in both the officer and the explorer. Up until now, the officer's words and actions have focused on the machine: he has been either explaining the machine or adjusting it. The explorer, in contrast, has been paying no attention to the machine and very little attention to what the officer has been saying. Now the explorer turns toward the machine, and the officer begins to pay closer attention to the explorer: "The officer had scarcely noticed the explorer's previous indifference, but he was now well aware of his dawning interest" (143). Even the condemned man, who has been "direct[ing] his gaze wherever the officer pointed a finger" (142), now also turns his attention to the explorer and copies his movements: "The condemned man imitated the explorer; since he could not use a hand to shelter his eyes he gazed upward without shade" (143). The officer stops "explaining to leave a space of time for quiet observation" (143). The distracted, indifferent observer now becomes an interested and engaged listener to the explanation of the machine. It is, in fact, the explorer who draws the officer back to his explanation with the expectant prompt, "Well, the man lies down" (143), with the implied question *And then what happens?*

When the officer explains that the machine begins to carry out the condemned man's sentence, the explorer asks what the sentence is. The officer is aghast that the explorer does not already know; apparently the new commandant was supposed to have informed the explorer about it. The explorer continues to ask a series of questions about the sentencing of the condemned man. The nature of the explorer's interest is important to note. The officer wants to explain the workings of the machine so that the explorer will understand what is happening during the execution, but the explorer is interested only in the judicial procedure preceding the execution. Just as earlier the explorer had commented on the officer's uniform "instead of making some inquiry about the apparatus as the officer had expected" (140), now the explorer asks about something other than what the officer expects, something other than the working of the apparatus. The explorer asks six questions about the sentence—about the wording of it, about what the condemned man knows about it and the fact that it has been passed, and about the man's opportunity for a defense against the charges that led to the sentence. Although the explorer has left behind his role as detached observer, he has not become the eager admirer of the machine that the officer wants him to be.

The explorer's body language also reveals his changing level of engagement. At the beginning of the story, he walks up and down with "almost visible indifference." When his interest in the cotton wool is sparked, he bends forward. When he is ready to hear the officer's explanation, he leans back and crosses his legs in ready anticipation. After he asks about the prisoner's sentence and intends to let the officer go on with his explanation, he leans back, as if satisfied with the answer given. But the gaze of the prisoner calls him to account, and he leans forward again: "The explorer intended to make no answer, but he felt the prisoner's gaze turned on him; it seemed to ask if he approved such goings-on. So he bent forward again, having already leaned back in his chair" (145). Finally, giving the first sign of his disapproval of the judicial procedure, he rises from his seat and says to the officer: "But he must have had some chance of defending himself" (145). At this point, he moves from the interrogative to the declarative, and in so doing moves from an observer to one who raises objections, albeit a weak one who is easily "pressed . . . back into his chair" (146). For as Rolleston points out, "his 'act' (standing up from the chair) is without consequence; he is speaking, as it were, for the record and does nothing to hinder the officer or interrupt him again."[9]

The sight of the prisoner brings on this change in role. The explorer's questions concerning the sentencing of the prisoner and what the prisoner knows about it sound as if the explorer is trying to learn whether the prisoner has received due process of law. Although, at the beginning of the story, he had been interested only in observation (and even in that not very strongly)—"for he traveled only as an observer" (151)—and indifferent toward the prisoner, the explorer now feels himself uncomfortably put into the role of the prisoner's advocate by the prisoner's gaze, even as the officer tries to put him in the role of the machine's advocate by his explanation. The explorer is not moved by sympathy for the plight of the prisoner—by all evidence he finds him irritating—but he seems to feel some responsibility to make sure there has been a proper legal procedure before the execution.

The explorer is not happy with the answers he receives about the sentencing of the prisoner: "The explanation of the judicial procedure had not satisfied him" (146). It is important to note that his dissatisfaction focuses on the *sentencing*, not the punishing, of the man, for this dissatisfaction occurs after the description of the machine's parts and the preparatory stages of the execution, but *before* the officer actually explains the writing work of the machine. The officer has mentioned the quivering of the machine and the fact that the prisoner will learn the law on his body, but the description of the gruesome process by which the law is written on his body is yet to come. It is not the method of punishment that the explorer disapproves of but the method of determining guilt, the trial, and the sentencing of the accused. But as Michael Wood poignantly asks, "Why is this violation of judicial procedure more extraordinary than the presence of a machine which tortures condemned men by writing on their flesh? Why is the officer smiling? A striking feature of the story is the tone or ordinary reasonableness in which what seem to be entirely unreasonable, indeed inhuman arrangements are discussed."[10]

The Scripting of Crime

In contrast to the detailed explanation the officer gives of the execution procedure, the description of the condemned man's "trial" is surprisingly brief. What takes up the space of a whole novel in Kafka's *The Trial* here takes the space of one sentence: "The captain came to me an hour ago, I wrote down his statement and appended the sentence to it" (146). Whereas Joseph K. knows at least that a charge of some sort has been made against him, even if he does not know what the charge is, prisoners in the penal colony are not informed that they have been charged, nor what the charge against them is; they do not know that they have been sentenced nor what their punishment is until they are brought before the apparatus. In *The Trial* "the crucial circumstance about K.'s trial is the fact that the charge against him is never specified. The existence of a guilt—some guilt—is assumed, but its nature is left undefined and remains unknown to both the protagonist and to the reader."[11] In the penal colony, however, the crucial circumstance of the prisoner's trial is the fact that the prisoner knows nothing until he is brought before the execution machine. He does not know which law he has been charged with breaking until, according to the officer, it is inscribed into his body.

For the officer, the explorer's inquiry into the judicial procedure is a distraction from the important issue—that the explorer understand the workings of the machine—just as the judicial procedure itself would be, were the officer to pursue it, a distraction from the important issue of the prisoner's coming to understand the law he has broken through the workings of the machine. The "simple" question of guilt and the "simple" process of sentencing are merely the precursors to the complex process of punishment, to the workings of the "very complex machine" (151) and the "hard task" (150) of the prisoner. The officer is interested in the *spectacle* of justice, in the aesthetic qualities of the smooth performance of the execution, not the meddling details of a judicial procedure that would only complicate things and slow them down.

But there is something even more disturbing, and more insidious, about the legal processes in this penal colony—something that readers seem to have missed: the condemned man's execution was scheduled before he even committed the crime! The officer tells the explorer, "I was quite near you *yesterday* when the commandant gave you the invitation. I heard him giving it" (155; emphasis mine). We know from the second sentence of the story that the invitation was "to witness the execution of a soldier condemned to death for disobedience and insulting behavior to a superior" (140); thus the crime was clearly specified. When the officer explains the process by which the condemned man has come to be standing in front of the apparatus awaiting his execution, he states,

> *Last night* the captain wanted to see if the man was doing his duty . . . there was his man curled up asleep. He took his riding whip and lashed him across the face. Instead of getting up and begging for pardon, the man caught hold of his master's leg, shook him and cried: "Throw that whip away or I'll eat you alive." That's the evidence. The captain came to me *an hour ago*, I wrote down his statement, and appended the sentence to it. Then I had the man put in chains. (146; emphases mine)

Thus the timetable for the whole process is as follows: *Yesterday* the commandant invited the explorer to the execution. *Last night* the crime occurred. And *an hour ago* the crime was reported, the charge made, and the sentence given. Not only is the crime committed after the execution has been scheduled but also there is only an hour between arrest and execution.

This is a more insidious legal system than even Joseph K. encounters: guilt is not only assumed but also created. An execution for disobedience and insulting behavior is scheduled, and then a soldier is placed in a situation in which he is likely to fail in his duties—having the senseless task of saluting a door every hour on the hour throughout the night when no one is there to see him do it. It is an execution in search of a man to condemn. Margot Norris points out that "the Law in the penal colony is . . . replaced by flimsy pretexts contrived to create an almost certain occasion for punishment (saluting a door every hour during the night),"[12] though she fails to note the prescheduling of the execution, which offers even more evidence of the staged and performative character of the whole penal colony.

Adding to the idea that the crime itself is staged—a part of the theater of the execution—is the glaring incongruity between the charges against the man and how he is depicted. In fact, we are told, he "looked so like a submissive dog that one might have thought he could be left to run free on the surrounding hills and would only need to be whistled for when the execution was due to begin" (140).[13] Further, the condemned man's purported outcry, "Throw that away or I'll eat you alive," is both comical in its absurdity and again completely at odds with the submissive character of the prisoner about to be executed. The officer tells the explorer that "guilt is never to be doubted" (145), a truism when the guilt itself is fabricated or staged. Norris identifies a whole host of ways in which the execution takes on the form of theater: "The officer, who has a passion for theater (like the Marquis de Sade), runs the execution like a one-man theater company, tending the props, giving stage directions, badgering a prospective patron to support a failing show, and eventually serving as an understudy for the lead."[14] All of this highlights the dramatic aspects of punishment in the penal colony, the performance of interpretation that the condemned man is made to give through his pain, and the staging of justice being done in spectacular and gruesome detail.

Of the process leading up to the execution, the officer says, "That was all quite simple" (146). For the officer, all cases are simple, and all are judged according to one guiding principle: "guilt is never to be doubted." His is the only court; no higher court exists: "Other courts cannot follow that principle, for they consist of several opinions and have higher courts to scrutinize them" (145). What other societies view as an important system of checks and balances, the officer views as a hindrance to the simple execution of justice. In keeping with the officer's one guiding principle of simplicity, one accusation is all that is necessary as evidence, all accused are guilty, and all sentences take the same form: the inscription of the law broken onto the condemned person's body. Theodor Adorno declares that "it is not the horrible which shocks, but its self-evidence."[15] It is the matter-of-factness with which the officer reports the legal proceedings, its self-evidence to him, that adds to the horror.

Like the world of the hermeneutical tyrant and the world of the father, the officer's court consists of one view—his own. His simple view of things, particularly of the prisoner's guilt, is much like Kafka's father's, who viewed his son's guilt as a simple matter. Kafka's father viewed his son's claim that he was afraid of him as a lie and an excuse for his behavior. Likewise the officer operates according to a hermeneutics not of suspicion but of dismissal, declaring that any answers the prisoner would give would be lies. As if to bring the discussion of the sentencing process to a close, the officer tells the explorer, "I've got him [the prisoner] and I won't let him go" (146), echoing Gregor's territorial claim on his framed, fur-muffed lady in "The Metamorphosis."

The officer says that his explanation will help the explorer "to follow the proceedings better" (142). However, the officer is confident about his assumptions concerning prisoners' guilt, but he is not quite sure of his powers of explanation: "Forgive me if my explanations seem rather incoherent" (144). This duty of explaining the judicial procedure was formerly carried out by the old commandant but has now fallen to the officer. The officer promises him, "You'll soon understand it" (142), and as the explanation proceeds, he asks the explorer, "Is that quite clear?" (146), "Can you appreciate now the work accomplished by the Harrow and the whole apparatus?" (149), and "Can you follow it?" (149). The frequency of the officer's questions underscores how important it is to him that the explorer understand the workings of the machine and understand them in the right way—as the infliction of justice, not torture.

The Performance of Punishment and Interpretation

The machine is, on one level, a means of public execution like any other—for example, the guillotine. It punishes an offender in a public arena, displacing the agency of revenge onto an apparatus, at the same time reinforcing the power of the government. The execution of the condemned man serves to reassure the rest of the community that justice, rather than lawlessness, reigns. Michel Foucault has shown the ways in which "the function of public torture and execution was to reveal the truth . . . a successful public execution justified justice, in that it published the truth of the crime in the very body of the man to be executed."[16]

However, this penal apparatus is unique in one significant respect. It literalizes the symbolic function of public execution such that the "truth of the crime," that is, the law broken, is quite literally "published . . . in the very body of the man": the law is literally engraved on his skin. While Foucault outlines the symbolic language of execution, Kafka literalizes that language in the penal apparatus. This literalization of figurative expressions, such as metaphors, Sokel argues, occurs frequently in Kafka's work, and "In the Penal Colony" is no exception:

> A decisive and profound experience is said to "leave a mark"; a lasting memory is "engraved" on one. Kafka's *The Penal Colony* depicts both metaphors as physical happenings. The penal machine slowly kills the condemned prisoner by literally engraving (German: *einkerben*) on his flesh the law he transgressed. He dies, in fact, remembering his lesson; "the mark left" by the law kills him.[17]

Thus, the penal apparatus literalizes both the symbolic language of public executions and the metaphors used to describe experiences of education and formation. The machine serves the public function of execution for the community and the personal function of "reforming" the condemned man: it simultaneously fulfills the functions of punishment that Foucault traces along a temporal continuum (or discontinuum) from punishment as vengeance to punishment as reform. That is, the apparatus imposes punishment as vengeance in killing the condemned man at the same time that it purportedly imposes punishment as reform in bringing the condemned to a point of enlightenment about the law he has broken.

According to the officer, it is a twelve-hour process: the first six hours of engraving prepare the prisoner to begin his interpretive process, which takes the next six. The officer tells the explorer that at the six-hour mark

> nothing more happens than that the man begins to understand the inscription, he purses his mouth as if he were listening. You have seen how difficult it is to decipher the script with one's eyes; but our man deciphers it with his wounds. To be sure, that is a hard task; he needs six hours to accomplish it. (150)[18]

Both the activity of the machine and the response of the man are described as hard work, the former as the hard work of writing, the latter as the hard work of reading and interpreting. The man's skin is the paper on which the text is written, and, according to the officer, his wounds become the means through which he reads the law, as well as the text itself.[19] Through this process, he learns the law he has broken; the execution functions as a process of enlightenment.

This process used to be, according to the officer, a huge public spectacle with hundreds of people in attendance; people arrived a day early to get a good view, and "fanfares roused the whole camp" (153). Requests for "front-row seats" were too numerous to fill, so "the Commandant in his wisdom ordained that children should have the preference" (154), a decision highlighting the execution's educational function for the community. As the condemned man deciphers the law, the community experiences justice being done. The condemned man is enlightened as to the nature of his crime, and the community is reaffirmed in its belief that the law is just and able to keep all in order. Foucault writes that

> it was the task of the guilty man to bear openly his condemnation and the truth of the crime he had committed. His body, displayed,

> exhibited in procession, tortured, served as the public support of a procedure that had hitherto remained in the shade; in him, on him, the sentence had to be legible for all.[20]

Foucault here refers to the punishment inflicted on the prisoner as symbolic of the sentence against him; this symbolism is made literal by the apparatus. The harrow is made out of glass so that the writing of the sentence is, in Foucault's phrase, "legible for all," even if the sentence itself cannot be read, except, allegedly, by the condemned man through his wounds. The community views the paying of the debt that revenge requires—"the judgment has been fulfilled" (150)—sees the reform of the prisoner in his experience of enlightenment—"how we all absorbed the look of transfiguration on the face of the sufferer" (154)—and is comforted by the impossibility of the crime being committed again as the machine lets the corpse fall "at the last into the pit with an incomprehensibly gentle wafting motion" (154).

Whereas Georg's sentence is figuratively written into him by his father, the prisoner's sentence is here literally inscribed onto and into him. And whereas Georg carries out his father's sentence *as if* the father's words have the power to compel his actions, the machine, as described by the officer, literally does have the power to compel action: the action of interpretive activity. Whereas Georg has his interpretive ability taken away from him, at least during the extent of their conversation, through his father's reinterpretation of everything that gave Georg power, the prisoner has interpretation forced upon him in a cruel subjugation of his interpretive capacity. In the penal colony, to interpret is to be in pain; to understand is to die. According to the officer's account, enlightenment comes not at the cost of excruciating pain but through it. The cost is much higher: life itself.

And yet, what sort of interpretation do we imagine the prisoner is engaging in as he undergoes torture? As Stanley Corngold asks, "What then is the status of the understanding that is given to the prisoner's faculty of reason (*der Verstand*) in the sixth hour?"[21] Surely someone who has been tortured to the point of being unable to speak does not have the mental capacity to decipher an ornate script that is illegible on paper, particularly when he must "read" it through his wounds. These questions raise doubts about the genre of the officer's narrative: is it an explanation of the workings of the machine, or an expression of his fantasy about what happens to the prisoner undergoing torture? In order to think more about this question, I turn to Levinas's essay "Useless Suffering" to reflect on the nature of the experience of pain and suffering.

Useless Suffering

Levinas's essay "Useless Suffering" can be read as an illustrative counter-narrative to the officer's description of the condemned man's experience in the machine. The first contrast between these two texts lies in the place that suffering has in their narratives. Contrary to the meager attention that the officer pays to the condemned man's pain, Levinas offers a dense phenomenology or detailed description of the experience of suffering. He dwells almost obsessively on it, as if grappling with language in order to offer his phenomenology. In contrast, the officer shows only passing interest in the pain inflicted by the machine and never recognizes it as suffering.

The officer gives indications of the excruciating nature of the pain the victim experiences, both through the description of the working of the machine and through details such as the fact that the man screams for two hours and then has no strength left to scream. But when he mentions the prisoner's pain, the officer refers to it as a side effect of, or a precursor to, the condemned man's act of interpretation: "The first six hours the condemned man stays alive almost as before, he only suffers pain" (149). The officer sees little difference between the state of the man before and during torture, as if the experience of torture were inconsequential. The presence of the word "only" is telling. Whereas Politzer argues that this line underscores that pain is unimportant to Kafka—"Kafka is true to his masochistic view of life when he minimizes the importance of physical suffering"[22]—the line actually underscores the reverse. There is a strong disjunction between, on the one hand, the content of what the officer is saying—that is, his description of pain—and, on the other, his attitude toward it, his complete indifference to it as suffering and his fascination with it as "enlightenment." In her book *The Body in Pain*, Elaine Scarry points out that "the most crucial fact about torture is that it is happening"[23] (or in this case about to happen), whereas for the officer the most crucial fact about the process he describes is that it is the means to the supposed enlightenment of the victim.

For the officer, the pain is merely part of the performance of punishment and justice. He laments the fact that he is no longer permitted to use an acid that increases the pain: "Nowadays the machine can no longer wring from anyone a sigh louder than the felt gag can stifle; but in those days the writing needles let drop an acid fluid, which we're no longer permitted to use" (154). In other words, the prisoner's performance is not as spectacular as it once was because his expressions of pain are no longer loud enough for those present to hear. In former days, "it was impossible to grant all the requests to be allowed to watch it nearby" (154). Such was the spectacle of the machine and its torture. In all of this, the condemned man's suffering is invisible—that is, of little importance and garnering no attention *as suffering*, even as his pain is a spectacle for all to watch and enjoy.

In Levinas's narrative, however, suffering is anything but invisible. For Levinas, the other's suffering of extreme pain must draw one's full attention when one is confronted with it. His intense focus on it draws his readers' attention away from all else to a concentration on what the experience of suffering is for the sufferer. Acknowledging that it is something experienced in consciousness, "similar to the lived experience of color, sound, contact, or any other sensation,"[24] Levinas suggests that it is unlike those experiences in that it is characterized by its unassumability. The sufferer cannot process or make sense of the experience of suffering, cannot assume it into her consciousness. Levinas describes the suffering of extreme pain as the "denial, the refusal of meaning, thrusting itself forward as a sensible quality" (91). He even goes so far as to describe it as "an in-spite-of-consciousness" (91), as the experience of the inability to process it in any way that would make sense of it. For Levinas suffering is experienced as the refusal or "revulsion" of meaning: it precludes the possibilities of enlightenment and is, in fact, marked by the experience of the impossibility of meaning.

Thus, while in the officer's account extreme pain is merely part of the very process by which an enhanced enlightenment occurs, for Levinas suffering is characterized by the very experience of being unable to assume, accept, receive, or process the experience one is undergoing. This inability to process the sensory data causing pain is not because there is too much sensation to process—it does not, he writes, "result from the excessive intensity of a sensation, from just some quantitative 'too much,' surpassing the measure of our sensibility and our means of grasping and holding" (91). In other words, suffering is not merely being overwhelmed by intense sensory data, as one might experience color that is excessively vibrant or noise that is excessively loud, to such an extent that one is unable to process that data. Rather, this unassumability of suffering is "an excess, an unwelcome superfluity, that is inscribed in a sensorial content, penetrating, as suffering, the dimensions of meaning that seem to open themselves to it, or become grafted onto it" (91).

The echoes of the officer's explanation of the machine ring loud in this passage. Reading this passage with his explanation in mind actually helps to unpack some of the density and opacity of Levinas's prose. The officer states that the ornate script of the law is inscribed into the prisoner's skin; Levinas describes suffering as an excess inscribed in sensory content, as if the excess inscribes the senses like the machine inscribes the prisoner's body. According to the officer, the machine's inscription finds its obverse in the reading work of the prisoner, resulting in his enlightenment; according to Levinas, the inscription of excess into the senses is experienced by the sufferer as the impossibility or rejection or refusal of meaning. Levinas writes that suffering is "the *way* in which the refusal, opposing the assemblage of data into a meaningful whole, rejects it" (91). Levinas describes a "backward consciousness . . . revulsion" (91). Thus, Levinas's dense phenomenology of suffering finds a visceral and visual contrast in the officer's description of the experience of the condemned man in the machine. The two narratives function as counterphenomenologies.

Related to this is the contrast in agency depicted by the officer and by Levinas. According to the officer, the condemned man is able to do something through what he endures that he was not able to do before: he is able to decipher the law. Even as he is subjected to torture, chained and enclosed by the machine, he somehow gains an enhanced agency that allows him to decipher the law he has purportedly broken, to "begin to understand" (150). It is, the officer tells the explorer, "a hard task"; the prisoner requires "six hours to accomplish it." The prisoner is not only able to do something he was not able to do before being put in the machine but also able to do something that most individuals, including the explorer, cannot do: the prisoner can decipher with his wounds what others cannot read with their eyes.

In contrast, Levinas draws our attention to the passivity of suffering, which is "more profoundly passive than the receptivity of our senses . . . an encounter more passive than experience" (92). Suffering is, he writes, "a pure undergoing" (92). The agency of the sufferer is not only *not* enhanced, *pace* the officer, it is destroyed. For in suffering, it is not merely that the individual's freedom is limited—the very capacity for freedom is destroyed. It is not that the sufferer is degraded to the point of having the "identity of a mere thing" (92) but that his identity, his agency, is dissolved by the suffering. Levinas writes that the sufferer's "humanity is overwhelmed by the evil that rends it, otherwise than by non-freedom: violently and cruelly, more irremissibly than the negation that dominates or paralyzes the act in non-freedom" (92). Thus it is not that the sufferer's agency is limited, or hampered, or reduced, or even brought to zero: it is obliterated in the process of suffering.

Finally, the starkest contrast between the two texts lies in the uses to which suffering is put and the meanings it is given. In the officer's narrative, the condemned man's pain is part of a public spectacle that performs justice for the community and reforms (through "education") and punishes the prisoner at the same time. Consequently, the condemned man's suffering as suffering is invisible; his pain is merely one aspect of a spectacle in which the highest levels of meaning take place at both the communal and individual levels. He tells the explorer, "Many did not care to watch it but lay with closed eyes in the sand; they all knew: Now Justice is being done. . . . How we all absorbed the look of transfiguration on the face of the sufferer, how we bathed our cheeks in the radiance of that justice, achieved at last and fading so quickly" (154). The officer describes a kind of communal ecstasy in response to the purported "transfiguration" of the sufferer who performs his role in the spectacle of justice. The sufferer is not so much someone in pain as someone undergoing the process of transfiguration and enlightenment for the benefit of the community. Thus, his suffering is useful, meaningful, and justified, according to the officer's narrative of it.

In contrast, Levinas declares that the suffering of an other (in other words, he is not talking about how I relate to or understand my own suffering) must remain useless to me. The moment I begin to find meaning in the other's suffering, to suggest that it has a purpose, whether communal or individual, I have crossed an ethical line. Any ascription of meaning to or use of another's pain is, according to Levinas, a further violence against her. Both individuals and communities make sense of suffering, inscribe it with meaning, or justify it. Levinas fits all of these under the term "theodicy," including both religious theodicies in which God has a supposedly good reason for our suffering and secular theodicies that justify evil and suffering on the basis of a greater good that comes out of them, such as, for example, the reform that is said to result from punishment. Levinas argues that these are all forms of justifying others' suffering, and he offers a powerful critique of such interpretational moves: "The justification of the neighbor's pain is certainly the source of all immorality" (99). The other's suffering must remain useless, unjustifiable, and unforgiveable to me—I must not try to make it useful or meaningful or in any way acceptable.

From this condemnation of using the other's suffering and the declaration that the other's suffering must remain useless to me, Levinas argues that attention to the suffering other is of prime importance. Rather than simply acknowledging the uselessness of the other's suffering, Levinas describes what he calls the interhuman order, which involves my attention to the suffering of the other, my suffering in response to it, and my responsibility to alleviate and eradicate the other's suffering. This attention to the suffering of the other—attention of the kind that desires to end or alleviate it, or what Levinas calls "the suffering of suffering, the suffering for the useless suffering of the other, the just suffering in me for the unjustifiable suffering of the other"—can be seen as "the supreme ethical principle, the only one it is impossible to question" (94). It is precisely this sort of attention that is strikingly absent in Kafka's story.

Levinas condemns any depiction of someone else's suffering that makes any use of it and proclaims attention to suffering—attention of the kind that seeks to stop or alleviate it—as the supreme ethical principle; the officer does just the opposite. He enthusiastically narrates the suffering of torture as being of supreme usefulness to both the individual and the community, offering an enviable enlightenment to the former and a radiant spectacle of justice to the latter. The current commandant's efforts to thwart this performance are viewed with hostility and disgust by the officer as he seeks to gain the explorer's support for his side.

By reading these two texts together, Levinas's dense language becomes easier to unpack, and we are able to understand more of what Levinas is trying to articulate about the unassumability, passivity, and uselessness of suffering. This is due in part to the officer's counteremphasis on the assumability, or readability, of the law for the condemned man; his *enhanced agency* of being able to read through his wounds; and the *usefulness* of this process of torture both in the condemned man's enlightenment and the community's assurance that justice is being done. Just as important is how Levinas helps us to read Kafka: reading Kafka's story with Levinas's emphasis on attention to suffering in mind highlights the failure of *any* character in Kafka's story to attend to suffering, respond with empathy, or try to alleviate it *in any way*. Though the story moves almost as a series of reports on what each character is paying attention to, none pays attention to suffering. Further, reading the officer's narrative with Levinas's condemnation of theodicy in mind helps us to resist the temptation of the officer's narrative—the temptation to believe in the usefulness of torture for the community and the tortured man himself. It is a temptation that the visiting explorer who is listening to the officer is unable to resist.

Scripting Suffering

Reading "In the Penal Colony" in tandem with Levinas's essay reveals that the hermeneutical tyranny of the officer takes another form in addition to his swift assumption of guilt and sentencing of the accused; it relates to his explanation of the victim's experience in the machine. The officer's description of the enlightenment that comes to the condemned man can be seen as a deliberate misinterpretation of the pain the man endures—an interpretive narrative that the explorer is being asked to buy into (as is the reader). There is no reason to believe that the officer's narrative describes the actual experience of a condemned man in the machine. It is a fantasy that the explorer and the reader are implicated in believing.

For it is only through the officer that we learn about the victim's ostensible experience of the machine. Would the interpretive nature of the condemned man's experience be obvious to the onlooker? The officer mentions that an ignorant onlooker would not be able to tell the difference made by the inscription of different laws. And the fact that the officer explains the machine so thoroughly to the explorer suggests that the spectacle is far from self-explanatory. Despite the claim that the machine works, after a few things are set up, "all by itself" (141), the officer's detailed explanation suggests that the viewer needs help in interpreting it. Though the machine is said to compel a prescribed interpretation from its victim, it is unable to do so in the uninitiated viewer. The officer's explanation gives the explorer an interpretive framework through which to understand the workings of the machine and the pain the condemned man suffers. However, there is little reason to believe that the apparatus has the effect on its victim that the officer suggests it does.

In fact, there is much in the story to suggest that the officer's narrative of the workings of the machine and its effects is itself another violent inscription of a "text" onto the condemned man's experience. The officer interprets the signs of pain on the victim's face as signs of his engagement in the enlightening process of interpretation, but might they be the signs of excruciating pain? The officer tells the explorer,

> But how quiet he grows at just about the sixth hour! Enlightenment comes to the most dull-witted. It begins around the eyes. From there it radiates. A moment that might tempt one to get under the Harrow oneself. Nothing more happens than that the man begins to understand the inscription, he purses his mouth as if he were listening. You see how difficult it is to decipher the script with one's eyes, but our man deciphers it with his wounds. To be sure, that is a hard task; he needs six hours to accomplish it. By that time the Harrow has pierced him quite through and casts him into the pit. (150)

By interpreting the facial expressions as indications of understanding, the officer inscribes the condemned man's suffering with meaning, redescribing it as the process of interpretation and enlightenment. The officer's inscription of meaning onto the condemned man's pain can be seen as an instance of hermeneutical tyranny, as the violent imposition of an interpretation presented as fact. He reinterprets the machine's actions as the hard task of writing and the victim's suffering as the hard task of interpretation, thereby inscribing meaning into the process of torture. While the machine inscribes the law onto the victim through a painful process, the officer inscribes meaning onto the painful process by reinterpreting it as interpretation.

Exquisite Torture and Plain Murder

Though the officer is the most glaring example of the failure to pay attention to suffering *qua* suffering paired with an elaborate justification of it, the explorer may be the most surprising and more important example—particularly because of his proximity to the perspective of the reader. On first glance, the explorer might strike the reader as merely an observer, the role in which the explorer likes to think of himself, or even as someone who disapproves of the officer's whole system rather than as someone who follows the officer's path of justifying suffering. However, a closer examination of two moments in the story reveals that the explorer is more of an accomplice to, and advocate for, the justification of suffering than it seems.[25]

When the officer asks the explorer to voice his support for the execution process to the new commandant of the colony, the explorer offers a rather minimal withholding of approval rather than outright condemnation. His initial response to the officer's request is a simple "No" (159), and then, "I do not approve of your procedure" (159). But this refusal does not come from his concern for the suffering inflicted by twelve hours of torture; it is, rather, the lack of an adequate judicial process before the execution that is of most concern to him. He has procedural rather than ethical concerns.

Further, he has no empathy for the condemned man and in fact finds him repulsive at several points. According to the story, he knew "from the very beginning . . . the answer he must give" (159) in response to the officer's request for his support for the machine, but the sight of the soldier and the condemned man makes him hesitate to give it. This hesitation is significant because it comes from the fact that he is touched by the "sincere conviction" (160) of the officer and repulsed by the actions of the other two, who are lapping up the warm rice pap, the condemned man with his tongue and the soldier with his "dirty hands" (154). The explorer is tempted, though only for "as long as it took to draw one breath" (159), to side with the officer.

Thus, he withholds his approval not out of a sense of sympathy for the condemned man, nor even out of a sense of outrage at the excruciating torture the machine inflicts. Though he is clear that it is an inhumane mode of execution, this has no emotional impact on him. Rather, it is his rational commitment to a certain idea of justice, in which the accused is given the opportunity to prove his innocence, that prevents him from offering his support to the officer and his system. Even though he asks numerous questions about the legal procedure leading up to the execution, he asks nothing about the operation of the machine itself. Though he thinks to himself that "the injustice of the procedure and the inhumanity of the execution were undeniable" (151), the explorer never exhibits a sense of outrage at the senseless infliction of inordinate pain. To stand before a machine of torture, and the human being on which it is about to be used, and to think that its inhumanity is merely undeniable—that is, not something one could convincingly declare humane—displays a lack of anything but an intellectual engagement in the process. The explorer himself underscores the compartmentalization of his ethical geography when he tells the officer, "Your sincere conviction has touched me, even though it cannot influence my judgment" (160).

That he is more concerned with the question of the legality of the proceedings than with the inhumanity of the punishment is clear from the fact that he does nothing to stop the officer's death. In fact, in one of the most disturbing moments in the story, the reader learns that the explorer approves of the officer's decision to put himself under the apparatus:

> If the judicial procedure were really so near its end—possibly as a result of his own intervention, as to which he felt himself pledged—then the officer was doing the right thing; in his place the explorer would not have acted otherwise. (163)

He both approves of the officer's decision and decides that were he the officer, he would do the same thing! Interestingly, this is the one moment in the story in which the explorer makes a moral judgment, and from that moment on he is no longer merely an observer. But his judgment raises numerous questions. Why is the officer's putting himself in the machine "doing the right thing"? How is it that the explorer can approve of the officer's decision even though he claims to consider the process of execution inhumane? And further, how is it possible that the explorer can go so far as to say that he would do the same thing in the officer's place? These are strong statements, particularly given that the strongest response to the judicial and penal procedure the explorer has been able to muster has been a mere withholding of approval.

The explorer reads the officer as a tragic hero, as the captain going down with his ship, and translates the officer's suicide into a noble gesture of loyalty. Once again things are being read as performances without any explicit recognition of their real costs. What is important is the symbolic nature of the officer's actions, their coherence with the narrative of the execution process to which he has committed himself, as if the officer were playing the lead role in a public drama, not the man responsible for the excruciating deaths of many and an unjust system. Both the officer and the explorer engage in a metaphorical interpretation of torture that obscures from vision the realities of the suffering it inflicts—a mode of interpretation common to torturers and the official discourse of torture.

Perhaps the most chilling line of the whole story occurs as the machine begins to kill the officer: "Because it was working so silently the machine simply escaped one's attention" (164). The officer's description of past crowds gorging on the spectacle of the condemned prisoner's experience of torture is certainly a disturbing image, but the image of the explorer standing next to the machine as it starts its gruesome work and paying it no attention is perhaps even more disturbing. While the officer is being jabbed with needles, the explorer is focused on the annoying antics of the prisoner. It is the sight of the prisoner and the soldier that "he [can] not bear" (164) rather than the sight of the officer being jabbed to death.

The explorer's annoyance with the prisoner and soldier, rather than horror at the process of torture going on right in front of him, reveals a striking displacement of attention and psychic engagement. That the explorer responds more strongly to the annoyances of the prisoner than to the functioning of a torture machine echoes the officer's oddly misplaced responses. For it is the conferences of the new commandant, "packed with spectators" and "turned into . . . public spectacles" (as the executions used to be) that make the officer "sick with disgust" (158) rather than the process of torture that he views with admiration. The officer's lack of disgust in response to the machine's gruesome work and lack of compassion for the victim stem from his fascination with the supposed enlightenment of the victim. The explorer's lack of compassion stems not from his involvement in the victim's pain but from his disengagement from it.

The explorer pays no attention to the officer—the suffering human being before him—once the machine starts. He stares at the machine for "quite a while" (164), without seeming to actually be paying any attention to it, since we are told that the "machine simply escaped one's attention" in the next sentence. His attention is soon drawn to the soldier and the condemned man, who are eagerly observing and pointing out different aspects of the workings of the machine. Any mention of the officer is glaringly absent. It is as if he were invisible, until his death. Even the officer's face in death underscores the absence of meaning: "No sign was visible of the promised redemption; what the others had found in the machine the officer had not found" (166). The absence of any description of the officer's experience of pain contrasts with the officer's elaborate depiction of the process the condemned man undergoes. Thus the story prevents the reader from interpreting the officer's experience in the machine as meaningful. No metaphorical reading of his death is possible here.

The explorer is not troubled when he considers the officer will be in the machine for twelve hours and then killed; he is troubled only when he realizes that the "machine [is] obviously going to pieces" (165). It is precisely because the machine turns out *not* to be torturing the officer that the explorer is troubled. He seems to have believed the officer's interpretation of the experience of the machine's victim as enlightenment, because he distinguishes between the officer's present experience of the machine and the experience other victims had of it: "This was no exquisite torture such as the officer desired, this was plain murder" (165). Once he realizes that the officer will not experience the enlightenment he has described, the explorer wants "to bring the whole machine to a standstill" (165).

What is particularly disturbing about the explorer's response is its implicit depiction of torture as something acceptable, even "exquisite," while swift death is "plain murder." When the explorer believes that the machine will put the officer through a process of torture that will contain a climactic point of hermeneutical enlightenment, the explorer thinks the officer has made the right choice in placing himself in the machine. When the machine is simply and swiftly killing the officer, the explorer feels compelled to stop the machine. The inscription of meaning into the process of torture through the interpretation of pain as the process of interpretation is revealed to be a fantasy seeking to obscure the violence of the machine. And it is a fantasy that the explorer has come to believe and even desire for the officer.

The explorer, who started out as an indifferent observer, has become implicated in the death of the officer through his belief in the officer's fantasy of meaningful and exquisite torture. The officer moves from the role of judge to condemned man, from the machine's advocate to its victim, from the one who explains the machine to the one who is unable to read its "writing"; the explorer moves from observer to advocate to judge to accomplice, from one who cannot read the ornate script the machine will write to one who is deeply troubled by the meaningless jabbing of the machine.

Four details reveal the explorer's alliance with the officer, despite his verbal statement to the contrary: his approval of the officer's decision to put himself in the machine, his failure to try in any way to stop him, his indifference to the initial workings of the machine, and his deep upset at the realization that the machine is not engaged in the long process of writing on the officer but rather is jabbing him to death. Had he been opposed to the workings of the machine, had he really considered it inhumane, he would have tried to prevent the officer's torture and death. The fact that he comes to the officer's aid only when it turns out he is *not* being tortured, as if this were a fate worse than death, reveals that he has fully imbibed the officer's fantasy of meaningful and useful suffering. Further, his pilgrimage to the old commandant's grave at the end of the story, his refusal to meet the mocking smiles of the men standing around it, and his remaining in place until the table has been pushed back over the grave also indicate his shift in allegiance. He has joined the party of the fantasy of meaningful torture and useful suffering.

In this book, I have argued that Kafka proposes a mode of interpretation that recognizes complexity and resists the temptation to simplify it; admits the contingency of its "arrivals" and eschews the claim to complete interpretation; acknowledges the possibility of multiple views; and allows for the possibility, even necessity, of revision of its own view. Interpretation of this sort seeks to engage in the effort to understand, rather than to control, the other, with its telos being not arrival but a drawing nearer to the other—proximity to, not power over, the other—and a deepening, though always partial, understanding of the other.

And yet interpretation—even interpretation of this sort—must not itself become tyrannical by claiming to be the only ethical mode of engagement with others. There are some situations in which our response to others should not take the form of interpretation, particularly a form of interpretation that translates an other's suffering metaphorically, such that the violence inflicted is obscured and the suffering undergone is translated into education or reform, or some other useful process that might justify it. Interpretation offers us a crucial mode of engagement with others, seeking to understand their complexity, acknowledge their views, and accept the possibility of revision and change over time in our interpretations and others', but we must also remain vigilant against the temptations of hermeneutical tyranny that Kafka so vividly portrays in his stories. This is particularly true when faced with others' suffering.

The reader of Kafka's "In the Penal Colony" could read the machine and its workings metaphorically, as representing something other than a machine of torture—and here there are a whole host of candidates for what the machine represents: writing itself, bureaucracy, the trial of writing *The Trial*, Kafka's excruciating struggles with Felice, "Old Testament" law, Christian sacrifice, and the list goes on. But might interpreting the machine in that way be to miss something the story is trying to teach us about the dangers of metaphorical readings, about the dangers of interpreting in such a way that we translate torture and suffering into less troublesome, less physical, less visceral, less obvious things? Interpreting the machine as, say, a metaphorical representation of writing requires setting aside the visceral details of the torture described—"the blood and vomit and sputum and muck and oil," what Corngold describes as the *excreta* of the story.[26] Might such a reading also fail to pay attention to the obsessive attention the story pays to what the characters themselves are and are not paying attention to? Might it be a reading that does not learn from the story's own enactments of reading and interpretation? Norris suggests that "critics too often see in Kafka's evocation of a golden age of penal severity . . . a nostalgia for apotheosized pain. Rather, his 'history,' like Nietzsche's ironic genealogy, exposes the falsehoods and deceptions that constitute the civilizing process . . . [the] Officer [is] robbed of a transcendence that was always fraudulent."[27] In response to the temptation readers have to erase through metaphor both torture and the physical suffering it inflicts, we would do well to echo Wood when he declares, "We can and must say that the condemned man doesn't read anything, he is just cruelly tortured in the name of a fastidious, verbally infatuated legality."[28]

In this chapter, I have tried to suggest that Kafka writes in such a way as to call our attention to suffering—to the physical, visceral, painful, excruciating suffering that the machine, were it to function as narrated, inflicts—and to the indifference to that suffering displayed by the characters in the story. To believe the officer's description of the workings of the machine as an accurate interpretation of what happens to the condemned man placed within it is to follow in the explorer's footsteps, to fall prey to the temptation of meaningful suffering. For as Corngold astutely points out, "This is not a story about true sentencing but about its disappearance in the intricacies and hollows of fiction. What we have had throughout is the narration of the reception on the part of the explorer, of a narrative produced by a fanatic of a ceremony."[29]

As Levinas teaches us, and as Scarry has shown, "physical pain does not simply resist language but actively destroys it."[30] Torture does not produce enlightenment; the infliction of extreme pain does not educate. And yet we seem to be able to spin elaborate narratives about its usefulness. Kafka's text calls us to resist repeating the tyranny of the officer by resisting the temptation to inscribe meaning into the machine's inscription of pain. In order to do so, we must actively interpret not the suffering but the tyranny, for interpretive activity can be a means to resist hermeneutical tyranny, not merely to replicate it.

A CONCLUDING NOTE

One of the most beautiful and moving passages in Kafka's oeuvre identifies the gap between the world and our perception of it:

> There has never been a time in which I have been convinced from within myself that I am alive. You see, I have only such a fugitive awareness of things around me that I always feel they were once real and are now fleeting away. I have a constant longing, my dear sir, to catch a glimpse of things as they may have been before they show themselves to me. I feel that then they were calm and beautiful. It must be so, for I often hear people talking about them as though they were.[1]

In this passage from one of Kafka's earliest extant works, "Conversation with the Supplicant," the young man, referred to as the supplicant, speaks of his sense of the contingency of things, their fleeting nature. Even he himself is of such a nature; he is never sure even that he is alive. Things around him move away just as he draws near. And yet there seems to be such stability, ease, and beauty in others' experience of the world, at least from how they speak of it. The supplicant communicates a longing to see as others see, to see what they see, but also to be seen by them—"It is the aim of my life to get people to look at me"[2]—for there is an isolation and loneliness to this man's relation to the world, as if he can never quite make contact with others or the things in the world.

In this book, I have suggested that how one views the world, and to what and how one pays attention, affects the mode of interpretation one uses to engage it. The world of the supplicant is so fleeting that he is reduced to merely longing for a glimpse of it, his sense of his own unreality so strong that he must try to get people to look at him, as if to affirm that he actually exists. In contrast, the hermeneutical tyrant, whether played by Kafka's father or one of the father/authority figures in his works, deems the world simple, amenable to his interpretations, and available for his mastery and fully at his disposal. Thus he interprets with confidence, and sometimes with little relation to what he is interpreting, since he has little need for accuracy. This also means that his interpretations are frequently destructive and sometimes violent.

The hermeneutical tyrant's impotent subject, often Kafka's protagonist, finds himself determined or destroyed by the tyrant's interpretation of him. Often he is filled with despair of any prospect of escape from the tyrant's hermeneutical power. In "The Judgment" and "The Metamorphosis," we witness the destructive results of hermeneutical tyranny. Georg's father usurps the very power of interpretation itself and reinterprets his son as a devilish human being and sentences him to death by drowning. Grete erases the ambiguity of Gregor's identity and resolves the hesitation that has kept the family from doing so earlier, so that the family can now eliminate him from their midst without guilt. The officer in "In the Penal Colony" reinterprets torture as the process of writing and pain as part of the process of deciphering, such that suffering is rendered invisible even though the whole event is a spectacle. These are some of the tyrants and victims we meet in Kafka's works.

Kafka's works depict battles between the tyrant and his despairing subject, but the mode of interpretation Kafka himself engages in and elicits from his reader is of another kind. In Kafka's "Letter to His Father," we see his emphasis on the partial nature of interpretations, the need to give space to other interpretations and views, acknowledge complexity and eschew the satisfactions of simplification. Kafka shows that multiple interpretations may more accurately represent something, like a complex relationship between father and son, than would a single one. Further, Kafka suggests that we recognize the limits of our abilities to fathom certain mysteries and complexities and find some measure of reassurance in arriving at a proximity to truth rather than its mastery.

Though Kafka's readers are no strangers to either despair or tyranny—both exist as temptations for anyone reading his work—they learn from Kafka's works themselves about another kind of interpretation, another kind of reading, another kind of engagement, what I have here called Kafka's ethics of interpretation. An examination of the interpretive activity in Kafka's stories reveals the destructive consequences of either hermeneutical tyranny or despair and brings out a challenge presented by the Kafkan text: to avoid the dangers implicit in either mode. The hermeneutical tyrant arrives at a definitive interpretation and thereby destroys the text, transforming it into what he has defined it to be, while the impotent subject ceases to interpret and thereby loses his identity as interpreter and sometimes his very life. One challenge of the Kafkan text, then, is to engage in ongoing interpretation and thus refrain either from arriving at a definitive or final interpretation, which would end the interpretive process, or from giving up on the interpretive process altogether. These are the poles of hermeneutic tyranny and despair.

Kafka's texts resist definitive, but inspire multiple, interpretations. They do not attempt to evade interpretation but rather disrupt the hermeneutical activity by which a text, or a person, is definitively interpreted. In so doing, they resist an activity that puts an end to interpretation. In reading Kafka's texts, the goal is not to arrive at the final interpretation, and thereby do away with the need for further interpretation. Nor is it to declare that interpretation is impossible. In order to be a good reader of Kafka's texts, one must be willing to engage in hermeneutical activity as an ongoing process, aware of the contingency of any one interpretation and aware that not to interpret or to end hermeneutical activity through a definitive interpretation leads to a destructive end, either for the text or for the (non)interpreter.

Interpretation is not inherently or necessarily violent. Some interpretations seek to justify violence, but interpretive activity can also be both a means to resist violence and a form of engagement with others. Kafka's breakdown of some of the standard categories and established boundaries by which we order the world—for example, the human and nonhuman forged in the character of Gregor Samsa or the convergence of the linguistic and the physical in the writing of the law in "In the Penal Colony"—challenges us to reexamine some of the ways in which we speak about identity and human nature, violence and power, language and interpretation. While the difficulty in interpreting Kafka's texts is experienced by each reader, the dangers of ceasing interpretive activity are enacted by his characters. All interpretations are not equal—some interpretations are closer to the text than others—but no interpretation has the right of a tyrant by which it can exclude all other interpretations as "mad, wild, *meshugge*, not normal."[3] That our attempts to interpret a text or a person can be destructive should give us pause and cause us to reflect on what we do as scholars involved in interpretive activity; that engaging in interpretation can be an important form both of resistance against violence and of engaging in the world more fully should give us impetus to proceed.

Paul Ricoeur suggests that "interpretation, philosophically understood, is nothing else than an attempt to make estrangement and distanciation productive."[4] Might interpretation, then, be a way for the supplicant to move toward the world, to catch the glimpse of things—perhaps we might even say, with Kafka, the "inner truth"—for which he longs? Might interpretation be a mode of engagement with others more likely to reassure him that he is alive than any antics by which he tries to get people to look at him? Kafka writes, "It's difficult to tell the truth, since there is only one truth, but that truth is alive and therefore has a lively, changing face."[5] This suggests that our hermeneutical activity itself must be lively and willing to accept that interpretation is not about an arrival once and for all but is, rather, a difficult and ongoing telling about that which keeps changing—a telling that might make our experiences of estrangement and distanciation both productive and less lonely, and might "reassure us . . . a little and make our living and our dying easier."[6]

NOTES

Introduction

1. Walter Benjamin, "Franz Kafka: On the Tenth Anniversary of His Death," in *Illuminations*, ed. Hannah Arendt, trans. Harry Zohn (New York: Schocken Books, 1968), 124.

2. Theodor W. Adorno, "Notes on Kafka," in *Can One Live after Auschwitz? A Philosophical Reader*, ed. Rolf Tiedemann, trans. Rodney Livingstone et al. (Stanford, Calif.: Stanford University Press, 2003), 212.

3. Harold Bloom, "Introduction," in *Franz Kafka's "The Metamorphosis,"* Modern Critical Interpretations (New York: Chelsea House, 1988), 4.

4. Clayton Koelb, *Kafka: A Guide for the Perplexed* (London: Continuum, 2010), 1.

5. Naomi Schor, "Fiction as Interpretation / Interpretation as Fiction," in *The Reader in the Text: Essays on Audience and Interpretation*, ed. Susan Suleiman and Inge Crosman (Princeton, N.J.: Princeton University Press, 1980), 170.

6. Franz Kafka, *Letter to His Father / Brief an den Vater*, trans. Ernst Kaiser and Eithne Wilkins (New York: Schocken Books, 1953), 125.

7. For example, Susan Sontag argues for the need for such defense when she equates interpretation with ravishment: "The work of Kafka, for example, has been subjected to a mass ravishment by no less than three armies of interpreters" (*Against Interpretation and Other Essays* [New York: Anchor Books, 1990], 13). Giorgio Agamben's *Idea of Prose* ends with a short piece titled "Kafka Defended against His Interpreters," which presents a parable-like discussion of explanations of the inexplicable (in *Idea of Prose*, trans. Michael Sullivan and Sam Whitsitt [Albany: SUNY Press, 1995], 137–38).

8. Sontag, *Against Interpretation*, 7.

9. Ibid., 13.

10. Stanley Corngold and Ruth Gross offer a different, more charitable reading of these interpretations: "Interpretations that might be characterized as theological, economic, biographical, existential, gender-political, psychoanalytic, neo-Gnostic, Marxian, and so on, have all proved rewarding in their own way" ("Introduction," in *Kafka for the Twenty-First Century* [Rochester, N.Y.: Camden House, 2011], 3).

11. J. Hillis Miller, "The Sense of an Un-Ending: The Resistance of Narrative Closure in Kafka's *Das Schloss*," in *Franz Kafka: Narration, Rhetoric, and Reading*, ed. Jakob Lothe, Beatrice Sandberg, and Ronald Speirs (Columbus: Ohio State University Press, 2011), 109.

12. Evelyn Torton Beck, *Kafka and the Yiddish Theater: Its Impact on His Work* (Madison: University of Wisconsin Press, 1971); Stanley Corngold, Jack Greenberg, and Benno Wagner, eds., *Franz Kafka: The Office Writings* (Princeton, N.J.: Princeton University Press, 2008); John Zilcosky, *Kafka's Travels: Exoticism, Colonialism, and the Traffic of Writing* (New York: Palgrave Macmillan,

2003); Hanns Zischler, *Kafka Goes to the Movies*, trans. Susan H. Gillespie (Chicago: University of Chicago Press, 2002).

13. Ritchie Robertson, *Kafka: Judaism, Politics, and Literature* (Oxford: Clarendon Press, 1985); Iris Bruce, *Kafka and Cultural Zionism: Dates in Palestine* (Madison: University of Wisconsin Press, 2007); June O. Leavitt, *The Mystical Life of Franz Kafka: Theosophy, Cabala, and the Modern Spiritual Revival* (New York: Oxford University Press, 2012).

14. Vivian Liska, *When Kafka Says We: Uncommon Communities in German-Jewish Literature* (Bloomington: Indiana University Press, 2009), 3.

15. Manfred Engel and Ritchie Robertson, eds., *Kafka und die Religion in der Moderne: Kafka, Religion, and Modernity* (Würzburg: Königshausen and Neumann, 2014).

16. Ritchie Robertson, *Kafka*, Brief Insights (New York: Sterling, 2004), and *Kafka: A Very Short Introduction*, Very Short Introductions (Oxford: Clarendon Press, 2004); Sander L. Gilman, *Franz Kafka*, Critical Lives (London: Reaktion, 2005); Saul Friedländer, *Franz Kafka: The Poet of Shame and Guilt*, Jewish Lives (New Haven, Conn.: Yale University Press, 2013).

17. Reiner Stach, *Kafka: The Decisive Years*, trans. Shelley Frisch (Orlando, Fl.: Harcourt, 2005), and *Kafka: The Years of Insight*, trans. Shelley Frisch (Princeton, N.J.: Princeton University Press, 2013); Nicholas Murray, *Kafka: A Biography* (New Haven, Conn.: Yale University Press, 2004).

18. Interestingly, two recent books draw our focus very concretely to the language of Kafka's works through the lens of translation: Michelle Woods, *Kafka Translated: How Translators Have Shaped Our Reading of Kafka* (New York: Bloomsbury, 2014), and Patrick O'Neill, *Transforming Kafka: Translation Effects*, German and European Studies (Toronto: University of Toronto Press, 2014). David Suchoff, *Kafka's Jewish Languages: The Hidden Openness of Tradition* (Philadelphia: University of Pennsylvania Press, 2011), also focuses on language, but rather than the languages of translation he looks at the influence of Yiddish and Hebrew on Kafka's works.

19. Liska's work draws a helpful connection between the study of Kafka's German-Jewish literary context and a focus on interpretation when she writes, "Kafka places his writings 'in the small world of German-Jewish literature,' . . . a world he defines in terms of multiple impossibilities, where the very idea of a firm place and solid ground becomes questionable. . . . German-Jewish literature should indeed not be regarded as a fixed and definable category or essence, but as the result of a focus, a set of questions asked in the process of reading and interpreting individual texts" (*When Kafka Says We*, 5–6).

20. Walter Benjamin, letter to Gershom Scholem, February 4, 1939, in *The Correspondence of Walter Benjamin and Gershom Scholem, 1932–1940*, ed. Gershom Scholem, trans. Gary Smith and Andre Lefevere (New York: Schocken Books, 1989), 240; emphasis in the original.

21. Robertson, *Kafka: Judaism, Politics, and Literature*; Karl Erich Grözinger, *Kafka and Kabbalah* (New York: Continuum, 1994).

22. Bruce, *Kafka and Cultural Zionism*, provides excellent resources for thinking about the Jewish cultural influences on Kafka and his works.

23. Grözinger, *Kafka and Kabbalah*, 1.

24. Harold Bloom, *The Strong Light of the Canonical: Kafka, Freud and Scholem as Revisionists of Jewish Culture and Thought*, City College Papers, no. 20 (New York, 1987), 3. The image of a Bloomian-Scholemian-Kafkan burrow from which one cannot find a way out arises here.

25. Bruce, *Kafka and Cultural Zionism*, 91.

26. James L. Kugel, *In Potiphar's House: The Interpretive Life of Biblical Texts* (Cambridge, Mass.: Harvard University Press, 1990), 2.

27. Daniel Boyarin, *Intertextuality and the Reading of Midrash* (Bloomington: Indiana University Press, 1990), viii.

28. David A. Frank, "Arguing with God, Talmudic Discourse, and the Jewish Countermodel: Implications for the Study of Argumentation," *Argumentation and Advocacy* 41 (Fall 2004): 85.

29. I am reminded here of Milan Kundera's *The Unbearable Lightness of Being* (New York: Harper and Row, 1984), which identifies two poles of unbearability—one light and one heavy—that could be correlated to these two poles of hermeneutical tyranny and hermeneutical despair.

30. For a discussion of the ethical turn in postmodernism, see my essay "Attending to Suffering in/at the Wake of Postmodernism," in *The Mourning After: Attending the Wake of Postmodernism*, ed. Neil Brooks and Josh Toth, 65–78 (Amsterdam: Rodopi, 2007).

31. Judith Butler, *Giving an Account of Oneself* (New York: Fordham University Press, 2005).

32. Anke Snoek, *Agamben's Joyful Kafka: Finding Freedom beyond Subordination* (New York: Bloomsbury, 2012), 2.

33. Ibid., 5.

34. Ibid., 6.

35. Beth Hawkins, *Reluctant Theologians: Kafka, Celan, Jabès* (New York: Fordham University Press, 2003), xvi; emphasis in the original.

36. Ibid., xxix.

37. Gilles Deleuze and Félix Guattari, *Kafka: Toward a Minor Literature*, trans. Dana Polan, Theory and History of Literature, vol. 30 (Minneapolis: University of Minnesota Press, 1986), 7; emphasis in the original.

38. Stach, *Kafka: The Years of Insight*, 294.

39. Kafka writes that the three stories—"The Stoker," "The Judgment," and "The Metamorphosis"—"belong together, both inwardly and outwardly. There is an obvious connection among the three, for which reason I would be reluctant to forgo the chance of having them published together in a book, which might be called *The Sons*" (letter to Kurt Wolff Verlag, April 11, 1915, in Franz Kafka, *Letters to Friends, Family, and Editors*, trans. Richard and Clara Winston [New York: Schocken Books, 1977], 96).

40. He writes, "I would really have preferred to publish a sizable collection of stories (let us say, the story from *Arkadia* ["The Judgment"], *The Metamorphosis*, and still another novella ["In the Penal Colony"]), under the collective title of *Punishments*" (letter to Kurt Wolff Verlag, October 15, 1915, ibid., 113). It is interesting to note, though, that when the proposal to publish just "The Judgment" and "In the Penal Colony" was presented, Kafka was strongly against it. He saw "The Metamorphosis" as a possible mediating text between them.

41. Benjamin, "Franz Kafka," 122.

42. It is important to note here that reading and interpreting Kafka are not always or even primarily marked by pleasure. There are strikingly funny moments in most of his work, clever irony that gives pleasure at its recognition, images and turns of phrase that bring admiration, but there are also gruesome details, painful moments, sad endings, disturbing images. As Kafka himself said, books can be like axes for the frozen seas within us—the hacking may be important but not necessarily pleasant. Thus, there are limitations to how far one might take Benjamin's metaphor, and dangers in its too-complete application.

43. Benjamin, "Franz Kafka," 124.

44. Walter H. Sokel, "The Programme of K.'s Court: Oedipal and Existential Meanings of *The Trial*," in *On Kafka: Semi-Centenary Perspectives*, ed. Franz Kuna (New York: Barnes and Noble, 1976), 21; emphasis mine.

Chapter 1

1. Kafka, *Letter to His Father*, 125. Subsequent references to this work will be made parenthetically in the text. Most translators translate *Geduldspiel* as "Chinese puzzle." I have dropped "Chinese" because its inclusion seems misleading. First, most readers will not know what a Chinese puzzle is, and second, the German word *Geduldspiel* has no Chinese connotation. Given that there are significant references to China elsewhere in Kafka's oeuvre, it would seem misleading to suggest that there is a connection here with those references. Of course, "puzzle" alone could give the impression of a mystery or unsolvable situation, which is precisely not what Kafka means here, but my discussion of its meaning should avoid that misconception.

2. Kafka's now oft-quoted line to Milena Jesenská that truth has a lively, changing face immediately comes to mind here.

3. Stach, *Kafka: The Years of Insight*, 294.

4. The German reads, "Du hast mich letzthin einmal gefragt, warum ich behaupte, ich hätte Furcht vor Dir" (6).

5. Note that Kafka's claim that he can provide only partial reasons for not answering his father's question mirrors his claim that he can give only a partial explanation of their relationship. In both cases, he resists the possibility of a complete interpretation or a complete explanation.

6. Sokel, "Programme of K.'s Court," 19.

7. Echoes of "The Metamorphosis" ring, of course, in this statement.

8. Peter Mailloux, *A Hesitation before Birth: The Life of Franz Kafka* (Newark: University of Delaware Press, 1989), 437.

9. Heinz Politzer, "Letter to His Father," in *Franz Kafka Today*, ed. Angel Flores and Homer Swander (Madison: University of Wisconsin Press, 1964), 226.

10. Stach, *Kafka: The Years of Insight*, 300.

11. Frederick J. Hoffman, "Escape from Father," in *The Kafka Problem*, ed. Angel Flores (New York: New Directions, 1946), 227.

12. Max Brod, *Franz Kafka: A Biography* (New York: Schocken Books, 1960), 23. Gershom Scholem, in a letter to Walter Benjamin of August 14, 1934, corroborates Kafka's depiction of his father: "By the way, everyone who knew Kafka personally reports that his father was in fact a figure like the one in 'The

Judgment.' He is said to have been especially contemptible and an unspeakable burden to his family" (Scholem, *Correspondence*, 137).

13. According to Ernst Kaiser and Eithne Wilkins's translation, Kafka seems to extend his inability to speak beyond the precincts of his father's presence when he writes, "What I got from you . . . was a hesitant, stammering mode of speech" (Kafka, *Letter to His Father*, 126). However, G. Humphrey Roberts's more accurate translation of this passage in Brod, *Franz Kafka*, "in your presence . . . I began to stammer and stutter" (23), and Brod's statement (in the chapter translated by Richard Winston), "When talking to anyone else . . . he talked absolutely freely, easily, elegantly, and with a winning wealth and flow of ideas that was often playful, always astoundingly natural, and anything but 'stammering'" (240), contradict Kaiser and Wilkins's extension.

14. Politzer, "Letter to His Father," 225.

15. Walter H. Sokel, "Kafka's Poetics of the Inner Self," in *Critical Essays on Franz Kafka*, ed. Ruth V. Gross (New York: Hall, 1990), 162.

16. The German reads, "Mein Schreiben handelte von Dir, ich klagte dort ja nur, was ich an Deiner Brust nicht klagen konnte" (Kafka, *Letter to His Father*, 86). My translation departs slightly from the Kaiser and Wilkins translation, which reads, "My writing was all about you; all I did there, after all, was to bemoan what I could not bemoan upon your breast" (87). Two reasons suggest the change in translation: First, it seems to me that the "all" added to the first part of the sentence is not warranted by the original and slightly changes the meaning of the sentence. For while Kafka's writing may have been, as he states, about his father, he does not say that it was *all* or *only* about his father. Second, the translation of "ich klagte dort ja nur" as "all I did there, after all, was to bemoan . . ." limits what Kafka did in his writing in a way that "I lamented there, after all, only . . ." does not. For Kafka suggests that what he lamented in his writing was what he would have lamented upon his father's breast, but he does not say that lamenting was the only thing he did in his writing. I believe these slight changes in translation are more faithful to the original German, resist simplifying what Kafka himself viewed in a very complex way, and suggest a wider range of possibilities for interpreting both Kafka's writing and his views of his writing. Thanks to Maruta Ray for her help with the translation issues related to this passage.

17. The image of the son upon the father's breast is reversed in "The Judgment" when the father lays his head upon his son's breast as Georg carries him to bed. The reversal is sinister in two ways: the father's gesture of intimacy and dependence is a precursor to his violent uprising, and the son's act of solicitude and caregiving is interpreted as an attempt to usurp his father's position. Kafka uses this image to describe his reading of Strindberg: "In a better state because I read Strindberg. . . . (I don't read him to read him, but rather to lie on his breast. He holds me on his left arm like a child. I sit there like a man on a statue. Ten times I almost slip off, but at the eleventh attempt I sit there firmly, feel secure, and have a wide view" [May 4, 1915, in Franz Kafka, *The Diaries of Franz Kafka, 1910–1923*, ed. Max Brod, trans. Joseph Kresh and Martin Greenberg with the cooperation of Hannah Arendt (1948; repr., New York: Schocken Books, 1975), 339]).

18. Letter to Milena Jesenská, July 4–5, 1920, in Franz Kafka, *Letters to Milena*, trans. Philip Boehm (New York: Schocken Books, 1990), 63.
19. John Urzidil, "Recollections," in Flores, *The Kafka Problem*, 22.
20. Frederick R. Karl, *Franz Kafka: Representative Man* (New York: Ticknor and Field, 1991), 604.
21. The German reads, "Du behauptest, ich mache es mir leicht, wenn ich mein Verhältnis zu Dir einfach durch Dein Verschulden erkläre" (120).
22. It is interesting to note that language connected to vermin again comes into play: "parasitism" and "preying."
23. Clayton Koelb, *Kafka's Rhetoric: The Passion of Reading* (Ithaca, N.Y.: Cornell University Press, 1989), 225.
24. Jill Robbins, *Prodigal Son / Elder Brother: Interpretation and Alterity in Augustine, Petrarch, Kafka, and Levinas* (Chicago: University of Chicago Press, 1991), 82.
25. Charles Bernheimer, *Flaubert and Kafka: Studies in Psychopoetic Structure* (New Haven, Conn.: Yale University Press, 1982), 52.
26. Koelb, *Kafka's Rhetoric*, 228.
27. Stach, *Kafka: The Decisive Years*, 294.
28. Pericles Lewis, *Religious Experience and the Modernist Novel* (Cambridge: Cambridge University Press, 2010), 141.
29. Sontag, *Against Interpretation*, 7.
30. September 23, 1912, in Kafka, *Diaries, 1910–1923*, 213.
31. Stach, *Kafka: The Decisive Years*, 210.
32. Walter H. Sokel, "Freud and the Magic of Kafka's Writing," in *The World of Franz Kafka*, ed. J. P. Stern (New York: Holt, Rinehart and Winston, 1980), 146.
33. For example, in a letter from November 1920, he told Milena Jesenská that he found the "therapeutic part of psychoanalysis a helpless mistake" (Kafka, *Letters to Milena*, 216).
34. Jacques Derrida, "Before the Law," in *Acts of Literature*, ed. Derek Attridge, 181–220 (New York: Routledge, 1992). See also Jacques de Ville's essay on Derrida's text, "On Law's Origin: Derrida Reading Freud, Kafka and Lévi-Strauss," *Utrecht Law Review* 7, no. 2 (April 2011): 77–92, where he elucidates what he sees as Derrida's articulation of another way Freud might be read with Kafka.
35. Adorno, "Notes on Kafka," 216.
36. Brod, *Franz Kafka*, 20.
37. Philip Rieff, *Freud: The Mind of the Moralist* (Chicago: University of Chicago Press, 1959), 105.
38. Karl, *Franz Kafka*, 604.
39. Sigmund Freud, *The Interpretation of Dreams: The Complete and Definitive Edition*, trans. and ed. James Strachey (New York: Basic Books, 2010), 121. There is a wonderful irony in the subtitle to this edition of Freud's text—its claim to completion and to being *the definitive* edition.
40. Ibid., 125.
41. Ibid., 130n2.
42. Ibid., 142.
43. Ibid., 142n2.
44. Ibid., 144.
45. Ibid., 144–45.

46. Ibid., 135n2.

47. Mark Edmundson, *Towards Reading Freud: Self-Creation in Milton, Wordsworth, Emerson, and Sigmund Freud* (Princeton, N.J.: Princeton University Press, 1990), 29. I am indebted to Edmundson's book for bringing this footnote to my attention.

48. Ibid.

49. Freud, *The Interpretation of Dreams*, 145.

50. Ibid., 528.

51. Gayatri Chakravorty Spivak, "Translator's Preface," in *Of Grammatology*, by Jacques Derrida (Baltimore: Johns Hopkins University Press, 1976), xlvi–xlvii.

52. Ibid., xlix.

53. Freud, *The Interpretation of Dreams*, 528.

54. Ibid.

55. Ibid.; emphasis in the original.

56. Theodor Adorno, *Prisms*, trans. Samuel Weber and Shierry Weber Nicholsen (Cambridge, Mass.: MIT Press, 1981), 250.

57. Adorno, "Notes on Kafka," 217.

58. Letter to Milena Jesenská, June 23, 1920, in Kafka, *Letters to Milena*, 55.

Chapter 2

1. Karl Erich Grözinger identifies "the most important finding" of his book as "the fact that Kafka's *Trial*, 'The Judgment,' 'In the Penal Colony,' and several other scattered fragments treating the theme of judgment were written under the direct influence of the Jewish High Holy Days, the 'Days of Awe.' . . . Wherever Kafka speaks in them of judgment, sin, atonement and justification, he is working from the direct context of a Jewish theology having to do with judgment and sin; in other words, from a religious context" (*Kafka and Kabbalah*, 183–84).

2. September 23, 1912, in Franz Kafka, *The Diaries of Franz Kafka, 1910–1913*, ed. Max Brod, trans. Joseph Kresh (New York: Schocken Books, 1965), 276.

3. Letter to Felice Bauer, June 2, 1913, in Franz Kafka, *Letters to Felice*, ed. Erich Heller and Jürgen Born, trans. James Stern and Elisabeth Duckworth (New York: Schocken Books, 1973), 265. It is important to note that Kafka goes on to engage in interpretive activity in relation to the story: "Now note this. Georg has the same number of letters as Franz, 'Bendemann' is made up of Bende and Mann, Bende has the same number of letters as Kafka, and the two vowels are also in the same place; out of pity for poor 'Bende,' 'Mann' is probably meant to fortify him for his struggles. 'Frieda' has the same number of letters as Felice; it also starts with the same letter; 'Friede' [peace] and 'Glück' [happiness, Latin *felicitas*] are also closely related; 'Brandenfeld,' owing to 'feld' [field], has some connections with 'Bauer' [peasant], and also starts with the same letter. And there are other similar things—all of which, needless to say, I only discovered afterwards" (265). Robert Alter connects Kafka's interpretive activity here to Jewish interpretive practices: "Every minute detail of the text, every vocable, is the marker of submerged meaning that the interpreter—even when he is the one from whom the text 'came out'—can only begin to guess. . . . Kafka is only a step away here from traditional Hebrew modes of exegesis such as *notarikon* (interpreting words as acrostics for sentences) and *gematria* (linking words with other words by reference to the numerical value of the constituent letters)" (*Necessary*

Angels: Tradition and Modernity in Kafka, Benjamin, and Scholem [Cambridge, Mass.: Harvard University Press, 1991], 71).

4. This lecture has been translated by both Loïc J. D. Wacquant and Matthew Adamson under the title "Social Space and Symbolic Power." Wacquant's translation appears in *Sociological History* 7, no. 1 (Spring 1989): 14–25. Adamson's translation, from which I quote here, is chapter 8 in Pierre Bourdieu, *In Other Words: Essays Towards a Reflexive Sociology* (Cambridge: Polity Press, 1990).

5. Bourdieu, *In Other Words*, 136.

6. Eric L. Santner, *My Own Private Germany: Daniel Paul Schreber's Secret History of Modernity* (Princeton, N.J.: Princeton University Press, 1996), 26.

7. John R. W. Speller offers a useful study of the connections between Bourdieu's theories and literary works, as well as the field of literature, in *Bourdieu and Literature* (Cambridge: Open Book, 2011). Speller argues that "literature also played an important role in the development of Bourdieu's theory. His key concept of field was first developed through his studies of literature, which determined its initial properties, and oriented its future applications" (18).

8. Loïc J. D. Wacquant, "Towards a Reflexive Sociology: A Workshop with Pierre Bourdieu," *Sociological History* 7, no. 1 (Spring 1989): 50.

9. Ibid.

10. Ibid. A frequent criticism of Bourdieu is, ironically, that he is overly theoretical, that his writing is both too abstract and too dense. Randall Collins, in *Sociology since Midcentury: Essays in Theory Cumulation* (New York: Academic Press, 1981), states, "Bourdieu is among the most empirically oriented of all the French intellectuals, but we must recognize that he is first of all an abstract theorist" (173). The discrepancy between Bourdieu's self-description as primarily not a theorist and others' description of him as "first of all an abstract theorist," while a potentially interesting subject of investigation, will not be taken up in this chapter.

11. Wacquant, "Towards a Reflexive Sociology," 50.

12. Ibid.

13. Pascale Casanova, *The World Republic of Letters*, trans. M. B. DeBevoise (Cambridge, Mass.: Harvard University Press, 2004), also brings Bourdieu and Kafka together but in a rather different way. By looking at the literary world as a social space, itself marked by inequalities, exclusions, major and minor players, Casanova historicizes Kafka, showing his position in a national and cultural context. She uses Bourdieu's work on the literary world to "describe the world republic of letters, which is to say the genesis and structure of international literary space," in order to develop a "new method for interpreting literary texts" (351) and a "new hermeneutic logic, at once specific—since it seeks to account for a text in its very singularity and literariness—and historical" (352). This new hermeneutic logic resists a universalization of Kafka that erases his ethnic, cultural, and national particularity. She argues that "the denial of hierarchical structure, of rivalry, of the inequality of literary spaces transforms the haughty regard of ethnocentric ignorance into either universalizing consecration or wholesale excommunication" (353).

14. Richard Jenkins, *Pierre Bourdieu*, Key Sociologists (London: Routledge, 1992), 84.

15. Bourdieu, *In Other Words*, 189.

16. Jenkins, *Pierre Bourdieu*, 98, quoting Bourdieu.

17. Franz Kafka, "The Judgment," trans. Willa and Edwin Muir, in Franz Kafka, *The Complete Stories*, ed. Nahum N. Glatzer (1946; repr., New York: Schocken Books, 1971), 78. Subsequent references to the story will be made parenthetically in the text.

18. Wacquant, "Towards a Reflexive Sociology," 39.

19. Thomas Luckmann and Peter Berger, "Social Mobility and Personal Identity," *European Journal of Sociology* 5 (1964): 335.

20. Letter to Felice Bauer, June 10, 1913, in Kafka, *Letters to Felice*, 267.

21. Kafka's letter to Felice following his public reading of "The Judgment" provides a startling parallel: "I took along your picture postcard from the party, and decided to let my hand rest on it quite quietly during the reading, and thus—by means of the simplest magic—have your support. But as the story began to take hold of me, I began at first to play with the card, then squeezed it and bent it without thinking. Just as well the card wasn't your dear hand; had it been, you wouldn't be able to write to me tomorrow, and that would have made it far too costly an evening for me" (ibid., 86). Georg tries to block Frieda's ability to speak; Kafka damages, in his imagination, Felice's hand and prevents her from writing.

22. Walter H. Sokel, "Perspectives and Truth in 'The Judgment,'" in *The Problem of "The Judgment": Eleven Approaches to Kafka's Story*, ed. Angel Flores (New York: Gordian Press, 1977), 207.

23. The translation of this passage by Joachim Neugroschel (in Franz Kafka, *The Metamorphosis and Other Stories: The Great Short Works of Franz Kafka*, ed. and trans. Joachim Neugroschel [New York: Charles Scribner's Sons, 1993], 63) reveals more clearly Frieda's resistance to Georg's attempt to censor her. The Muirs translate the passage as follows: "When, breathing heavily under his kisses, she was still able to add, 'All the same, it does upset me.'" The German reads, "Wenn sie dann, rasch atmend unter seinen Küssen, noch vorbrachte: 'Eigentlich kränkt es mich doch'" (Franz Kafka, *Sämtliche Erzählungen* [Frankfurt am Main: Fischer, 1993], 25).

24. Kafka, *Diaries, 1910–1913*, 296. Kafka dedicated this story to Miss Felice B. and called it her story.

25. Sokel, "Perspectives and Truth," 217.

26. The important relation between newspapers and power is discussed in the next chapter in connection with "The Metamorphosis."

27. Pierre Bourdieu, "Flaubert's Point of View," trans. Priscilla Parkhurst Ferguson, *Critical Inquiry* 14, no. 3 (Spring 1988): 541.

28. Sokel, "Perspectives and Truth," 208.

29. Bourdieu, "Social Space and Symbolic Power," 16.

30. Santner identifies this transformation as the most dramatic in the story: "No doubt the most breathtaking scene of the whole story involves the father's sudden mutation from frail and childlike dependent to death-bringing tyrant" (*My Own Private Germany*, 130).

31. This passage sounds remarkably similar to Kafka's account of his father's response to his latest engagement: "She probably put on a fancy blouse, something these Prague Jewesses are good at, and right away, of course, you decided to marry her. And as fast as possible, in a week, tomorrow, today" (Kafka, *Letter to His Father*, 107).

32. This, too, is echoed in Kafka's letter to his father, when he writes of his father's offering to give him "advice about how [he] could go in for these things [sexual relations] without danger." Kafka writes, "So there was hardly any smudge of earthly filth on you at all. And it was you who pushed me down into this filth—just as though I were predestined to it—with a few frank words . . . the filth began with me" (ibid., 105).

33. In "The Metamorphosis," Herr Samsa fills his pockets with apples with which to overcome Gregor; he drives him back into the room with them, wounding him with one that gets lodged in Gregor's back in the process. As a verminous insect, Gregor has no possibility of possessing pockets and, thus, of possessing power. In Kafka's letter to his father, while taking on his father's voice in the rejoinder, Kafka writes, "To make life comfortable for yourself without worries and without self-reproaches, you prove that I have taken your fitness for life away from you and put it in my own pocket" (ibid., 123).

34. In Kafka's letter to his father, he suggests that the furthest regions of the map are the only ones that hold out the possibility of escape from the father, but it turns out that Georg's father's power reaches even to the vast wilderness of Russia.

35. Walter H. Sokel, *Franz Kafka*, Columbia Essays on Modern Writers (New York: Columbia University Press, 1966), 18–19.

36. Jenkins, *Pierre Bourdieu*, 155; emphasis in the original.

37. Ibid., 154–55, quoting Bourdieu. Here Bourdieu emphasizes that what we say is often not only a form of communication but also a means of exercising authority.

38. Bourdieu, *In Other Words*, 189.

39. Bernheimer, *Flaubert and Kafka*, 182.

40. See Herbert Tauber, *Franz Kafka: An Interpretation of His Works* (New Haven, Conn.: Yale University Press, 1948), for more on the father as a divine judge.

41. Peter Berger, "Towards a Sociological Understanding of Psychoanalysis," *Social Research* 32, no. 1 (Spring 1965): 37.

42. Bourdieu, *In Other Words*, 149.

43. Ibid., 136.

44. Kafka, *Letter to His Father*, 27.

45. Butler, *Giving an Account of Oneself*, 48.

46. Letter to Felice Bauer, June 2, 1913, in Kafka, *Letters to Felice*, 265–66.

47. Note that Georg addresses his parents as a unit as if they were not separated by death. This reinforces that his actions are no longer directed by his father's power over him.

48. Sokel, *Franz Kafka*, 231.

49. Ibid.

50. Similarly, as Butler notes, the father also seems to suffer a reversal: "When the father condemns the son, the father himself collapses on the bed with a large sound, as if the condemnation had struck him down as well. . . . The father, in condemning the son, also condemned himself" (*Giving an Account of Oneself*, 45).

51. Brod, *Franz Kafka*, 129.

52. Butler, *Giving an Account of Oneself*, 60.

53. Ibid.

54. Letter of December 4–5, 1912, in Kafka, *Letters to Felice*, 86–87. Note that this "inner truth" recalls Freud's unplumbable point.

55. Letter to Milena Jesenská, June 23, 1920, in Kafka, *Letters to Milena*, 55.

56. Letter to Kurt Wolff Verlag, August 19, 1916, in Kafka, *Letters to Friends*, 126.

Chapter 3

1. Franz Kafka, *The Metamorphosis*, trans. and ed. Stanley Corngold (New York: Norton, 1996), 3. Subsequent references to this work will be made parenthetically in the text.

2. Tzvetan Todorov, *The Fantastic: A Structuralist Approach to a Literary Genre*, trans. Richard Howard (Cleveland, Ohio: Press of Case Western Reserve University, 1973), 169.

3. Michael Wood, *Literature and the Taste of Knowledge* (Cambridge: Cambridge University Press, 2005), 68.

4. Todorov, *The Fantastic*, 169.

5. Ibid.; emphasis mine.

6. Ibid.

7. Ibid., 172; emphasis mine.

8. Ibid., 173.

9. Ibid., 172; emphasis mine.

10. James Rolleston, *Kafka's Narrative Theater* (University Park: Pennsylvania State University Press, 1974), 68.

11. Ibid., 141.

12. David Eggenschwiler, "'The Metamorphosis,' Freud, and the Chains of Odysseus," in *Franz Kafka*, ed. Harold Bloom, Modern Critical Interpretations (New York: Chelsea House, 1986), 202.

13. Walter H. Sokel, "From Marx to Myth: The Structure and Function of Self-Alienation in Kafka's *Metamorphosis*," in Bloom, *Franz Kafka's "The Metamorphosis,"* 111.

14. Dean Swinford, who also engages Todorov's discussion of the fantastic in relation to "The Metamorphosis," suggests a parallel with Kafka's readers, who, he argues, look away from Gregor's verminous form *so that* they can interpret him: "Interpretation of 'The Metamorphosis' has historically deemphasized the form of Samsa's body in relation to the various concepts it purportedly signifies. This interpretation has resulted in a hermeneutics that overlooks the bug in pursuit of its elusive significance" ("The Portrait of an Armor-Plated Sign: Reimagining Samsa's Exoskeleton," in *Kafka's Creatures: Animals, Hybrids, and Other Fantastic Beings*, ed. Marc Lucht and Donna Yarri [Lanham, Md.: Lexington Books, 2010], 213). On a similar note, but focusing on Gregor's hybrid identity rather than his verminous form, Melissa De Bruyker argues that "Kafka's stories stage immanent audiences who observe and turn away from hybrid animals in order to decrease complexity or reach a stage of apparent rational (human) behavior" ("Who Identified the Animal? Hybridity and Body Politics in Kafka's 'The Metamorphosis' and *Amerika* [*The Man Who Disappeared*]," in Lucht and Yarri, *Kafka's Creatures*, 204).

15. De Bruyker argues that hybrids, "characters combining human with animal features," "signal a crisis situation in which distinctions between human and

animal, notions like subjectivity and humanity and modes of observation are at stake" ("Who Identified the Animal?," 191).

16. Wolfgang Iser, *The Implied Reader: Patterns of Communication in Prose Fiction from Bunyan to Beckett* (Baltimore: Johns Hopkins University Press, 1974), 280, 283.

17. Ibid., 285.

18. Ibid., xiv.

19. Ibid.

20. This line is strikingly similar to the possessive claim the officer in Kafka's "In the Penal Colony" makes about the prisoner to be condemned: "I've got him and I won't let him go" (in Kafka, *The Complete Stories*, 146).

21. The father's tight-fitting uniform reappears in "In the Penal Colony" in the officer's "tight-fitting full-dress uniform coat" (ibid., 142).

22. Franz Kafka, "The Judgment," trans. Willa and Edwin Muir, ibid., 81.

23. It is interesting to note that the cane the father uses is actually the office manager's, which he has left behind on his swift retreat. That Gregor's superior's cane is used by his father to drive him into his room echoes the fact that his father has tricked Gregor into his enslavement to the firm by pretending that the family does not have enough money to pay their debt. In both cases, the power of the firm is used by the father to corner Gregor into an unpleasant situation.

24. In fasting not out of principle but because he cannot find the food he craves, Gregor foreshadows Kafka's hunger artist.

25. Walter H. Sokel, "Education for Tragedy," in *Franz Kafka's "The Metamorphosis,"* ed. Stanley Corngold (New York: Bantam, 1972), 179.

26. Stanley Corngold, "Kafka's Manuscript Revisions," in Kafka, *The Metamorphosis*, 55.

27. Mark Lucht argues that there is much at stake, more broadly, in maintaining the distinction between human and animal: "The demonstration of the conventionality or arbitrariness of the distinction between human and animal would reveal the moral stakes at play in the maintenance of that distinction—we distinguish ourselves from animals ontologically in order to justify our use of them as resources—as well as the connections between human dominance of animals and patriarchal, aristocratic, oligarchic, and colonialist power structures" ("Introduction," in Lucht and Yarri, *Kafka's Creatures*, 7).

28. In doing so, Grete also unties the moral responsibility that binds them to Gregor. Lucht draws a connection between our claims to be distinct from animals and our treatment of others, human and nonhuman: Kafka, he suggests, "seems to have recognized that the ways in which we represent ourselves as human, and distinguish ourselves from others human and animal, shape our conduct in morally significant ways, and that human comportment with respect to nonhuman animals is closely connected with the manner in which we treat other people" (ibid., 9).

29. Letter to Grete Bloch, April 21, 1914, in Kafka, *Letters to Felice*, 394–95.

30. Harold Bloom, *The Anxiety of Influence* (Oxford: Oxford University Press, 1973), 5.

31. In contrast to Gavriel Ben-Ephraim, who also attends to the hermeneutical conundrum that Gregor's identity constitutes for the reader, I would argue that it is not as he claims, that "the insect always is and is not Gregor" that constitutes "one of the most difficult of the story's cognitive dissonances," but rather that

Gregor always is insect and human. It is the very inability to say "is not" to either identity that creates the cognitive dissonance. See Gavriel Ben-Ephraim, "Making and Breaking Meaning: Deconstruction, Four-Level Allegory, and 'The Metamorphosis,'" *Midwest Quarterly* 35, no. 4 (Summer 1994): 450–68.

32. Sokel, "From Marx to Myth," 115.

33. Rolleston, *Kafka's Narrative Theater*, 141.

34. Eggenschwiler, "'The Metamorphosis,'" 216.

35. Letter to Felice Bauer, December 6–7, 1912, in Kafka, *Letters to Felice*, 89.

36. Ibid.

37. Corngold notes this passage as the final among several other details that suggest that this is most likely a Catholic family (*Franz Kafka's "The Metamorphosis"* [New York: Bantam, 1972], 40n9).

38. Sokel, "From Marx to Myth," 112.

39. Maurice Blanchot, *The Work of Fire*, trans. Charlotte Mandell (Stanford, Calif.: Stanford University Press, 1995), 10.

40. Todorov, *The Fantastic*, 167. Subsequent references to this work will be made parenthetically in the text.

41. I am indebted to Walter Sokel for pointing this out to me.

42. Charles Bernheimer, "On Death and Dying: Kafka's Allegory of Reading," in *Kafka and the Contemporary Critical Performance: Centenary Readings*, ed. Alan Udoff (Bloomington: Indiana University Press, 1987), 367.

43. January 24, 1922, in Kafka, *Diaries, 1910–1923*, 405.

Chapter 4

1. Giorgio Agamben seems to follow in this line of thought when he declares that the machine is language itself (*Idea of Prose*, 115).

2. Stanley Corngold, "Allotria and Excreta in 'In the Penal Colony,'" in *Lambent Traces: Franz Kafka* (Princeton, N.J.: Princeton University Press, 2004), 68.

3. Kafka, *The Complete Stories*, 140. Subsequent references to this work will be made parenthetically in the text.

4. The phrase "almost visible" is intriguing, suggesting that the narrator is able to see things that are invisible to other characters but also that there is a category of things that are bounded by, or situated in the space between, the visible and the invisible on either side. What makes something *almost* visible, rather than invisible or barely visible? The phrase recalls Kafka's statement that he is a hesitation before birth—the moment before appearance—as well as a passage from "Conversation with the Supplicant" in which the speaker wishes he could see things as they are just before they present themselves to him: "I have a constant longing, my dear sir, to catch a glimpse of things as they may have been before they show themselves to me" (Franz Kafka, "Description of a Struggle," in *The Penal Colony: Stories and Short Pieces*, trans. Willa and Edwin Muir [New York: Schocken Books, 1948], 14).

5. For an account of Kafka's interest in fashion, see Mark M. Anderson, *Kafka's Clothes: Ornament and Aestheticism in the Habsburg Fin de Siècle* (Oxford: Clarendon Press, 1992). He writes, "Kafka's own writings, with their repeated references to fashion, elegant clothing, uniforms, and fur, revealed a surprisingly acute sense for the 'superficial' spectacle of urban life" (1). Also of interest, Anderson notes that Kafka's father ran a "clothing accessories store in Prague

that carried fancy goods (*Galanteriewaren*) such as silk handkerchiefs, lace, buttons, slippers, parasols, and the like" (2).

6. See *Heath's German and English Dictionary*, rev. Karl Breul (Boston: Heath, 1906), 154. I refer to this dictionary, published in Kafka's lifetime, to show that the arcane meaning of *die Egge* was in play at the time.

7. *The American Heritage College Dictionary*, 3rd ed. (Boston: Houghton Mifflin, 1993), 1238.

8. Whenever things become unusually large in Kafka's stories, it is a good idea to take note. The father in "The Judgment" appears a giant of a man and throws his enormous newspaper in Georg's direction; Gregor's father wields a heavy newspaper and speaks in a voice that sounds like a whole host of fathers.

9. Rolleston, *Kafka's Narrative Theater*, 92.

10. Wood, *Literature*, 82.

11. Sokel, "Programme of K.'s Court," 1.

12. Margot Norris, "Sadism and Masochism in 'In the Penal Colony' and 'A Hunger Artist,'" in *Reading Kafka: Prague, Politics, and the Fin de Siècle*, ed. Mark Anderson (New York: Schocken Books, 1989), 175.

13. As in *The Trial*, the one about to be executed is compared to a dog.

14. Norris, "Sadism and Masochism," 175.

15. Adorno, "Notes on Kafka," 215.

16. Michel Foucault, *Discipline and Punish: The Birth of the Prison*, trans. Alan Sheridan (New York: Vintage, 1979), 44.

17. Sokel, *Franz Kafka*, 5–6. As Sokel points out, this literalization of figurative language echoes the literalization of metaphor that takes place in Gregor's metamorphosis, where the common insult, "he's vermin," becomes literally true.

18. Stanley Corngold has pointed out a potential problem with the Muirs' translation of this passage, arguing that their translation of *entziffern* as "understand," rather than "decipher," offers a false depiction of "the status of the understanding that is given to the prisoner's faculty of reason (*der Verstand*) in the sixth hour" ("Allotria and Excreta," 77) and "encourag[es] the reader to conclude that the victim's 'understanding the inscription' in the sixth hour is the same thing as his apprehending through reason the truth of an ethical commandment" (77). Corngold argues that it is not the script itself that the prisoner understands but the fact that there is a script to be deciphered.

19. Thanks to Emily Gravett for pointing out that the wounds are themselves also the text.

20. Foucault, *Discipline and Punish*, 43.

21. Corngold, "Allotria and Excreta," 77.

22. Heinz Politzer, *Franz Kafka: Parable and Paradox*, rev. ed. (Ithaca, N.Y.: Cornell University Press, 1966), 100.

23. Elaine Scarry, *The Body in Pain: The Making and Unmaking of the World* (New York: Oxford University Press, 1988), 9.

24. Emmanuel Levinas, "Useless Suffering," in *Entre Nous: Thinking-of-the-Other*, trans. Michael B. Smith and Barbara Harshav (New York: Columbia University Press, 1998), 91. Subsequent references to this work will be made parenthetically in the text.

25. Because of this, I would have to redirect Michael Wood in his searching self-criticism when he writes, "I find I am so troubled by the traveller's sympathy

for the officer and by Kafka's meticulous attention to the officer's smile, that I risk underrating the traveller's action in opposing the procedure" (*Literature*, 86). Instead I would suggest that Wood risks underrating the explorer's complicity with the procedure by overlooking the ways he, in fact, becomes its supporter.

26. Corngold, "Allotria and Excreta," 68.

27. Norris, "Sadism and Masochism," 172.

28. Wood, *Literature*, 89.

29. Corngold, "Allotria and Excreta," 80.

30. Scarry, *The Body in Pain*, 4.

A Concluding Note

1. Franz Kafka, "Conversation with the Supplicant," in Franz Kafka, *The Penal Colony: Stories and Short Pieces*, trans. Willa and Edwin Muir (New York: Schocken Books, 1948), 14.

2. Ibid., 12.

3. Kafka, *Letter to His Father*, 21.

4. Paul Ricoeur, *Interpretation Theory: Discourse and the Surplus of Meaning* (Fort Worth: Texas Christian University Press, 1976), 44.

5. Letter to Milena Jesenská, June 23, 1920, in Kafka, *Letters to Milena*, 55.

6. Kafka, *Letter to His Father*, 125.

WORKS CITED

Adorno, Theodor W. "Notes on Kafka." Translated by Samuel Weber and Shierry Weber Nicholsen. In *Can One Live after Auschwitz? A Philosophical Reader*, edited by Rolf Tiedemann, translated by Rodney Livingstone et al., 211–39. Stanford, Calif.: Stanford University Press, 2003.

———. *Prisms*. Translated by Samuel Weber and Shierry Weber Nicholsen. Cambridge, Mass.: MIT Press, 1981.

Agamben, Giorgio. *Idea of Prose*. Translated by Michael Sullivan and Sam Whitsitt. Albany: SUNY Press, 1995.

Alter, Robert. *Necessary Angels: Tradition and Modernity in Kafka, Benjamin, and Scholem*. Cambridge, Mass.: Harvard University Press, 1991.

The American Heritage College Dictionary. 3rd ed. Boston: Houghton Mifflin, 1993.

Anderson, Mark M. *Kafka's Clothes: Ornament and Aestheticism in the Habsburg Fin de Siècle*. Oxford: Clarendon Press, 1992.

———, ed. *Reading Kafka: Prague, Politics, and the Fin de Siècle*. New York: Schocken Books, 1989.

Beck, Evelyn Torton. *Kafka and the Yiddish Theater: Its Impact on His Work*. Madison: University of Wisconsin Press, 1971.

Ben-Ephraim, Gavriel. "Making and Breaking Meaning: Deconstruction, Four-Level Allegory and 'The Metamorphosis.'" *Midwest Quarterly* 35, no. 4 (1994): 450–68.

Benjamin, Walter. "Franz Kafka: On the Tenth Anniversary of His Death." In *Illuminations*, edited by Hannah Arendt, translated by Harry Zohn, 111–40. New York: Schocken Books, 1968.

Berger, Peter. "Towards a Sociological Understanding of Psychoanalysis." *Social Research* 32, no. 1 (Spring 1965): 26–41.

Bernheimer, Charles. *Flaubert and Kafka: Studies in Psychopoetic Structure*. New Haven, Conn.: Yale University Press, 1982.

———. "On Death and Dying: Kafka's Allegory of Reading." In Udoff, *Kafka and the Contemporary Critical Performance*, 87–96.

Blanchot, Maurice. *The Work of Fire*. Translated by Charlotte Mandell. Stanford, Calif.: Stanford University Press, 1995.

Bloom, Harold. *The Anxiety of Influence*. Oxford: Oxford University Press, 1973.

———, ed. *Franz Kafka*. Modern Critical Interpretations. New York: Chelsea House, 1986.

———, ed. *Franz Kafka's "The Metamorphosis."* Modern Critical Interpretations. New York: Chelsea House, 1988.

———. *The Strong Light of the Canonical: Kafka, Freud and Scholem as Revisionists of Jewish Culture and Thought*. City College Papers, no. 20. New York, 1987.

Bourdieu, Pierre. "Flaubert's Point of View." Translated by Priscilla Parkhurst Ferguson. *Critical Inquiry* 14, no. 3 (Spring 1988): 539–62.

———. *In Other Words: Essays Towards a Reflexive Sociology*. Cambridge: Polity Press, 1990.

———. "Social Space and Symbolic Power." Translated by Loïc J. D. Wacquant. *Sociological History* 7, no. 1 (Spring 1989): 14–25.

Boyarin, Daniel. *Intertextuality and the Reading of Midrash*. Bloomington: Indiana University Press, 1990.

Brod, Max. *Franz Kafka: A Biography*. New York: Schocken Books, 1960.

Bruce, Iris. *Kafka and Cultural Zionism: Dates in Palestine*. Madison: University of Wisconsin Press, 2007.

Butler, Judith. *Giving an Account of Oneself*. New York: Fordham University Press, 2005.

Casanova, Pascale. *The World Republic of Letters*. Translated by M. B. DeBevoise. Cambridge, Mass.: Harvard University Press, 2004.

Collins, Randall. *Sociology since Midcentury: Essays in Theory Cumulation*. New York: Academic Press, 1981.

Corngold, Stanley, ed. *Franz Kafka's "The Metamorphosis."* New York: Bantam, 1972.

———. *Lambent Traces: Franz Kafka*. Princeton, N.J.: Princeton University Press, 2004.

Corngold, Stanley, Jack Greenberg, and Benno Wagner, eds. *Franz Kafka: The Office Writings*. Princeton, N.J.: Princeton University Press, 2008.

Corngold, Stanley, and Ruth V. Gross. "Introduction." In *Kafka for the Twenty-First Century*, edited by Stanley Corngold and Ruth V. Gross, 1–23. Rochester, N.Y.: Camden House, 2011.

De Bruyker, Melissa. "Who Identified the Animal? Hybridity and Body Politics in Kafka's 'The Metamorphosis' and *Amerika* (*The Man Who Disappeared*)." In *Kafka's Creatures: Animals, Hybrids, and Other Fantastic Beings*, edited by Marc Lucht and Donna Yarri, 191–210. Lanham, Md.: Lexington Books, 2010.

Deleuze, Gilles, and Félix Guattari. *Kafka: Toward a Minor Literature*. Translated by Dana Polan. Theory and History of Literature, vol. 30. Minneapolis: University of Minnesota Press, 1986.

Derrida, Jacques. "Before the Law." In *Acts of Literature*, edited by Derek Attridge, 181–220. New York: Routledge, 1992.

———. *Of Grammatology*. Translated by Gayatri Chakravorty Spivak. Baltimore: Johns Hopkins University Press, 1976.

De Ville, Jacques. "On Law's Origin: Derrida Reading Freud, Kafka and Lévi-Strauss." *Utrecht Law Review* 7, no. 2 (April 2011): 77–92.

Edmundson, Mark. *Towards Reading Freud: Self-Creation in Milton, Wordsworth, Emerson, and Sigmund Freud*. Princeton, N.J.: Princeton University Press, 1990.

Eggenschwiler, David. "'The Metamorphosis,' Freud, and the Chains of Odysseus." In Bloom, *Franz Kafka*, 199–219.

Engel, Manfred, and Ritchie Robertson, eds. *Kafka und die Religion in der Moderne: Kafka, Religion, and Modernity*. Würzburg: Königshausen and Neumann, 2014.

Flores, Angel, ed. *The Kafka Problem*. New York: New Directions, 1946.

Flores, Angel, and Homer Swander, eds. *Franz Kafka Today*. Madison: University of Wisconsin Press, 1964.
Foucault, Michel. *Discipline and Punish: The Birth of the Prison*. Translated by Alan Sheridan. New York: Vintage, 1979.
Frank, David A. "Arguing with God, Talmudic Discourse, and the Jewish Countermodel: Implications for the Study of Argumentation." *Argumentation and Advocacy* 41 (Fall 2004): 71–86.
Freud, Sigmund. *The Interpretation of Dreams: The Complete and Definitive Edition*. Translated and edited by James Strachey. New York: Basic Books, 2010.
Friedländer, Saul. *Franz Kafka: The Poet of Shame and Guilt*. Jewish Lives. New Haven, Conn.: Yale University Press, 2013.
Geddes, Jennifer L. "Attending to Suffering in/at the Wake of Postmodernism." In *The Mourning After: Attending the Wake of Postmodernism*, edited by Neil Brooks and Josh Toth, 65–78. Amsterdam: Rodopi, 2007.
Gilman, Sander L. *Franz Kafka*. Critical Lives. London: Reaktion, 2005.
Gross, Ruth V., ed. *Critical Essays on Franz Kafka*. New York: Hall, 1990.
Grözinger, Karl Erich. *Kafka and Kabbalah*. New York: Continuum, 1994.
Hawkins, Beth. *Reluctant Theologians: Kafka, Celan, Jabès*. New York: Fordham University Press, 2003.
Heath's German and English Dictionary. Revised by Karl Breul. Boston: Heath, 1906.
Hoffman, Frederick J. "Escape from Father." In Flores, *The Kafka Problem*, 214–46.
Iser, Wolfgang. *The Implied Reader: Patterns of Communication in Prose Fiction from Bunyan to Beckett*. Baltimore: Johns Hopkins University Press, 1974.
Jenkins, Richard. *Pierre Bourdieu*. Key Sociologists. London: Routledge, 1992.
Kafka, Franz. *The Complete Stories*. Edited by Nahum N. Glatzer. Translated by Edwin and Willa Muir. 1946. Reprint, New York: Schocken Books, 1971.
———. *The Diaries of Franz Kafka, 1910–1913*. Edited by Max Brod. Translated by Joseph Kresh. New York: Schocken Books, 1965.
———. *The Diaries of Franz Kafka, 1910–1923*. Edited by Max Brod. Translated by Joseph Kresh and Martin Greenberg with the cooperation of Hannah Arendt. New York: Schocken Books, 1975.
———. *Letters to Felice*. Edited by Erich Heller and Jürgen Born. Translated by James Stern and Elisabeth Duckworth. New York: Schocken Books, 1973.
———. *Letters to Friends, Family, and Editors*. Translated by Richard and Clara Winston. New York: Schocken Books, 1977.
———. *Letters to Milena*. Translated by Philip Boehm. New York: Schocken Books, 1990.
———. *Letter to His Father / Brief an den Vater*. Translated by Ernst Kaiser and Eithne Wilkins. New York: Schocken Books, 1953.
———. *The Metamorphosis*. Translated and edited by Stanley Corngold. New York: Norton, 1996.
———. *The Metamorphosis and Other Stories: The Great Short Works of Franz Kafka*. Edited and translated by Joachim Neugroschel. New York: Charles Scribner's Sons, 1993.
———. *The Penal Colony: Stories and Short Pieces*. Translated by Willa and Edwin Muir. New York: Schocken Books, 1948.

———. *Sämtliche Erzählungen*. Frankfurt am Main: Fischer, 1993.
Karl, Frederick R. *Franz Kafka: Representative Man*. New York: Ticknor and Field, 1991.
Koelb, Clayton. *Kafka: A Guide for the Perplexed*. London: Continuum, 2010.
———. *Kafka's Rhetoric: The Passion of Reading*. Ithaca, N.Y.: Cornell University Press, 1989.
Kugel, James L. *In Potiphar's House: The Interpretive Life of Biblical Texts*. Cambridge, Mass.: Harvard University Press, 1990.
Kundera, Milan. *The Unbearable Lightness of Being*. New York: Harper and Row, 1984.
Leavitt, June O. *The Mystical Life of Franz Kafka: Theosophy, Cabala, and the Modern Spiritual Revival*. New York: Oxford University Press, 2012.
Levinas, Emmanuel. "Useless Suffering." In *Entre Nous: Thinking-of-the-Other*, translated by Michael B. Smith and Barbara Harshav, 91–101. New York: Columbia University Press, 1998.
Lewis, Pericles. *Religious Experience and the Modernist Novel*. Cambridge: Cambridge University Press, 2010.
Liska, Vivian. *When Kafka Says We: Uncommon Communities in German-Jewish Literature*. Bloomington: Indiana University Press, 2009.
Lucht, Marc. "Introduction." In *Kafka's Creatures: Animals, Hybrids, and Other Fantastic Beings*, edited by Marc Lucht and Donna Yarri, 3–16. Lanham, Md.: Lexington Books, 2010.
Luckmann, Thomas, and Peter Berger. "Social Mobility and Personal Identity." *European Journal of Sociology* 5 (1964): 331–44.
Mailloux, Peter. *A Hesitation before Birth: The Life of Franz Kafka*. Newark: University of Delaware Press, 1989.
Miller, J. Hillis. "The Sense of an Un-Ending: The Resistance of Narrative Closure in Kafka's *Das Schloss*." In *Franz Kafka: Narration, Rhetoric, and Reading*, edited by Jakob Lothe, Beatrice Sandberg, and Ronald Speirs, 108–22. Columbus: Ohio State University Press, 2011.
Murray, Nicholas. *Kafka: A Biography*. New Haven, Conn.: Yale University Press, 2004.
Norris, Margot. "Sadism and Masochism in 'In the Penal Colony' and 'A Hunger Artist.'" In Anderson, *Reading Kafka*, 170–86.
O'Neill, Patrick. *Transforming Kafka: Translation Effects*. German and European Studies. Toronto: University of Toronto Press, 2014.
Politzer, Heinz. *Franz Kafka: Parable and Paradox*. Rev. ed. Ithaca, N.Y.: Cornell University Press, 1966.
———. "Letter to His Father." In Flores and Swander, *Franz Kafka Today*, 221–37.
Ricoeur, Paul. *Interpretation Theory: Discourse and the Surplus of Meaning*. Fort Worth: Texas Christian University, 1976.
Rieff, Philip. *Freud: The Mind of the Moralist*. Chicago: University of Chicago Press, 1959.
Robbins, Jill. *Prodigal Son / Elder Brother: Interpretation and Alterity in Augustine, Petrarch, Kafka, and Levinas*. Chicago: University of Chicago Press, 1991.
Robertson, Ritchie. *Kafka*. Brief Insights. New York: Sterling, 2004.
———. *Kafka: A Very Short Introduction*. Very Short Introductions. Oxford: Clarendon Press, 2004.

———. *Kafka: Judaism, Politics, and Literature*. Oxford: Clarendon Press, 1985.

Rolleston, James. *Kafka's Narrative Theater*. University Park: Pennsylvania State University Press, 1974.

Santner, Eric L. *My Own Private Germany: Daniel Paul Schreber's Secret History of Modernity*. Princeton, N.J.: Princeton University Press, 1996.

Scarry, Elaine. *The Body in Pain: The Making and Unmaking of the World*. New York: Oxford University Press, 1988.

Scholem, Gershom, ed. *The Correspondence of Walter Benjamin and Gershom Scholem, 1932–1940*. Translated by Gary Smith and Andre Lefevere. New York: Schocken Books, 1989.

Schor, Naomi. "Fiction as Interpretation / Interpretation as Fiction." In *The Reader in the Text: Essays on Audience and Interpretation*, edited by Susan Suleiman and Inge Crosman, 165–82. Princeton, N.J.: Princeton University Press, 1980.

Snoek, Anke. *Agamben's Joyful Kafka: Finding Freedom beyond Subordination*. New York: Bloomsbury, 2012.

Sokel, Walter H. "Education for Tragedy." In Corngold, *Franz Kafka's "The Metamorphosis,"* 169–86.

———. *Franz Kafka*. Columbia Essays on Modern Writers. New York: Columbia University Press, 1966.

———. "Freud and the Magic of Kafka's Writing." In *The World of Franz Kafka*, edited by J. P. Stern, 145–58. New York: Holt, Rinehart and Winston, 1980.

———. "From Marx to Myth: The Structure and Function of Self-Alienation in Kafka's *Metamorphosis*." In Bloom, *Franz Kafka's "The Metamorphosis,"* 105–16.

———. "Kafka's Poetics of the Inner Self." In Gross, *Critical Essays on Franz Kafka*, 157–73.

———. "Perspectives and Truth in 'The Judgment.'" In *The Problem of "The Judgment": Eleven Approaches to Kafka's Story*, edited by Angel Flores, 193–237. New York: Gordian Press, 1977.

———. "The Programme of K.'s Court: Oedipal and Existential Meanings of *The Trial*." In *On Kafka: Semi-Centenary Perspectives*, edited by Franz Kuna, 1–21. New York: Barnes and Noble, 1976.

Sontag, Susan. *Against Interpretation and Other Essays*. New York: Anchor Books, 1990.

Speller, John R. W. *Bourdieu and Literature*. Cambridge: Open Book, 2011.

Spivak, Gayatri Chakravorty. "Translator's Preface." In Derrida, *Of Grammatology*, ix–lxxxvii.

Stach, Reiner. *Kafka: The Decisive Years*. Translated by Shelley Frisch. Orlando, Fl.: Harcourt, 2005.

———. *Kafka: The Years of Insight*. Translated by Shelley Frisch. Princeton, N.J.: Princeton University Press, 2013.

Suchoff, David. *Kafka's Jewish Languages: The Hidden Openness of Tradition*. Philadelphia: University of Pennsylvania Press, 2011.

Swinford, Dean. "The Portrait of an Armor-Plated Sign: Reimagining Samsa's Exoskeleton." In *Kafka's Creatures: Animals, Hybrids, and Other Fantastic Beings*, edited by Marc Lucht and Donna Yarri, 211–36. Lanham, Md.: Lexington Books, 2010.

Tauber, Herbert. *Franz Kafka: An Interpretation of His Works*. New Haven, Conn.: Yale University Press, 1948.
Todorov, Tzvetan. *The Fantastic: A Structuralist Approach to a Literary Genre*. Translated by Richard Howard. Cleveland, Ohio: Press of Case Western Reserve University, 1973.
Udoff, Alan, ed. *Kafka and the Contemporary Critical Performance: Centenary Readings*. Bloomington: Indiana University Press, 1987.
Urzidil, John. "Recollections." In Flores, *The Kafka Problem*, 20–24.
Wacquant, Loïc J. D. "Towards a Reflexive Sociology: A Workshop with Pierre Bourdieu." *Sociological History* 7, no. 1 (Spring 1989): 26–63.
Wood, Michael. *Literature and the Taste of Knowledge*. Cambridge: Cambridge University Press, 2005.
Woods, Michelle. *Kafka Translated: How Translators Have Shaped Our Reading of Kafka*. New York: Bloomsbury, 2014.
Zilcosky, John. *Kafka's Travels: Exoticism, Colonialism, and the Traffic of Writing*. New York: Palgrave Macmillan, 2003.
Zischler, Hanns. *Kafka Goes to the Movies*. Translated by Susan H. Gillespie. Chicago: University of Chicago Press, 2002.

INDEX